ESCAPE PATH LIGHTING

ESCAPE PATH LIGHTING

A NOVEL

John Newton

Victoria University of Wellington Press

Victoria University of Wellington Press
PO Box 600, Wellington
New Zealand
vup.wgtn.ac.nz

A catalogue record is available from the
National Library of New Zealand.

ISBN 9781776562336

Printed by Blue Star, Wellington, New Zealand

'He . . . wore a shirt on various Polynesian themes
and dating from the Truman administration.'

Thomas Pynchon, *The Crying of Lot 49*

DRAMATIS PERSONAE

MANFRED SINGLETON, an avant-garde composer
MARIGOLD INGLE, a herbalist
CHUCKLES (Chuck), a parrot, Marigold's familiar
ARTHUR BARDRUIN, a poet

At the BPWF
SIGRID TUPELO, an endocrinologist
JONAH (Joe) BRAVO, a retired scholar, husband of
    Sigrid
JUANITA DÍAZ, a Lacanian psychoanalyst
WANDA BLISSBALL, a yoga instructor
CHRISTIAN BOGDANOVIC
JUSTIN ANODYNE   } poetry instructors
HARRIET WHITBREAD
WILLOW DURST, an intern
FRANK HORTUNE, a musician, in treatment with
    Juanita

At Shady Grove
BRIDGET O'DWYER, a hospitality worker
GROOBER, a family man
COOCH, a meth-head, partner of Groober

MARLEY
CASSIDY } children of Cooch and Groober
QUINN
LEO, a fisherman
BUNG-EYE BEN, a recreational brewer
HOMEBAKE, a three-legged cur

MEI-LIN CHIN, an apprentice poet
WILLIAM CHANG, an apprentice poet

WIREMU (Koro Bill) TE PATU, a grocer
JUNE TE PATU, a fly-tier, wife of Koro Bill
JUAN & CONCHITA, baristas
SIMON RICHWHITE, an architect
BIG WAYNE
LITTLE WAYNE } elderly bikers
SHANE
ZANE
PAULIE LAULALA, a deck hand
WIKI LAULALA, a hospitality worker, wife of Paulie
CAPTAIN BLOOD, a poetry lover
MIRIAMA, a hospitality worker
SLIPPERY BOB, a mandolinist
BLUEY WINTERS, VANESSA THRUSH, party guests
CONSTABLE DAVE, an officer of the law
CAITLIN ZINGER, a journalist
LEILANI JONES, the island's mayor

BOOK 1

CHAPTER 1

How much Manfred Singleton can see is
subject to dispute. No one on sleepy
Rock Oyster Island has ever observed
him without his shades, cumbersome Aristotle
Onassis numbers, with lenses like the butt ends
of plus-sized Heinekens. Mind you, Manfred
keeps to himself, he's not the sort of person
you meet at the store. Talk to the locals,
you'll learn there's a lot not to know about him.
Like where he got four million bucks (give or
take) for a concrete monstrosity by Richwhite &
Crotch. Like whether the godawful squealing
noise that he pipes from a sound system
hidden in the spinifex really is some kind
of 'difficult' music or just meant to scare
the little shits who throw stones on his roof.
Cranky old Manfred! Where would the gossips
at the Bali Hai Tearooms be without him?
Just as well, really, they can't see him now.
What kind of creep (they might plausibly ask)
needs to wear military night-vision goggles
to stare at himself in a mirror in

a darkened room? A room that resembles
an underground bunker, or some dire
modernist concert hall: off-form concrete,
mean leather couches, electronic
keyboards, a mixing desk. And a portable
clothes rack, on which he first tidily
hangs up his jacket and Hugo Boss shirt,
and then wheels aside to gaze neutrally
at the insensate void where his breasts
used to be. No one would call him a clubbable
fellow, you can't blame the locals for
having their doubts. But fear not, amiable
reader: Manfred sees everything.

✦

On the darkened headland, across the bay
at the Blue Pacific Wellness Farm,
scented tealights in thick glass tumblers
burn on the doorsteps of two dozen cedar
chalets. In 500-thread-count Egyptian cotton
the worried well sleep their dreamless sleep:
the well fed, the well stretched, the well
scrubbed and mud-bathed and rubbed and exfoliated,
punctured and pampered, heard and affirmed,
the chakra-balanced, the colonically
irrigated . . . Only the patients of
Juanita Díaz, Analista Lacaniana
(late of Buenos Aires, by way of Melbourne,
Australia), enjoy visitations through
the Gate of Horn. Dr Díaz insists
on this, and her patients know better than to

disappoint her. Likewise Sigrid Tupelo,
her quondam lover and co-director;
and so, for that matter, Sigrid's husband,
cactus fancier, de-frocked scholar
and tacit third partner in the BPWF,
ex-professor Jonah (Joe) Bravo. Not
that Juanita is fierce, exactly, but both
would agree she's 'particular'. She is also,
Joe has just been reflecting, apropos
of something she was almost about to
say, quite possibly the most opaque
woman he has ever nursed a crush on.
This, mind you, with no disrespect to
Sigrid – Griddle, as he calls her in fun;
also Gridiron, Grid-search, Gridlock, Two
Pillow, Tuppence, and pet names more banal
still – a severely perplexing woman in
her own right. It is midnight in what is
informally known as the Farmhouse (a.k.a.
Sigrid and Joe's), at the kitchen table
of which the three partners have been
knocking off a notable Malbec by Enrique
Foster. Juanita, now set to call it a night,
bestows her *buenas noches* kisses
and heads up the slope through the olives
to her separate quarters. 'Something's
bothering her,' says Joe, as he rounds up
the glasses and rinses them off. 'It's always a bad
sign when Nita stays late.' Sigrid looks up
from her spreadsheet. 'Yes, I thought so too.'

⨖

The clinker-built dinghy rows like a bathtub
but Marigold Ingle doesn't care.
When she digs on the oars she can feel her
core body converting the water's inertia
to thrust. It makes her feel powerful like
nothing she knows: as strong as the make-believe
father whose hippie hands crafted it.
In the glare of the headlamp, garfish,
suspended, ride above the seagrass like slender
blue rods. The spotlight undoes them: held
by its gaze, they wait for the dip net
she slides underneath them. She does her work
crisply – a dozen is plenty – turns off
the spotlight, lies back and lets the boat drift.

Her mother – her lovely Aquarian name,
Persia, that's what she always called her –
nights like this they'd play Constellations,
inventing their own: the Sunfish, the Cowboy Hat.
The stars haven't changed. Or the smell of
the seagrass, drying in wave-sculpted ridges
along the high-tide mark. Commuters have come,
of course, overseas money, estates on
the headlands (helipads, ground staff with tasers).
But the gully: it's much as it was when
they bought it – Persia and Sonny, in that
cheap scruffy decade – except, today,
greener and better loved. Or so Marigold
imagines . . . after all, it's only a story.
The fact is, she can't picture Sonny
at all, and even when Persia got sick
she was still just a teen. She remembers

them only in this life that she lives:
the dinghy, the garden, the alcohol.
The remedies. The kindnesses. And in
the tireless delight that keeps everything
contained, that no one has ever dug
deep enough to find the other side of.
A leaping mullet falls with a slap, then
another: there must be a kingfish about.
But now a small breeze comes snuffling;
she's no longer warm, as she slips the oars
back in the rowlocks, takes a grip on the water.

⚔

As the evening winds down at
the Sandgroper Lounge, the action reverts
to the pleasure craft moored offshore.
'Come and party with us, babe,' the punters
implore as they trip from the bar –
the pleasantry aimed at a comely young
woman with a glossy black bob, a short
leather skirt and a T-shirt announcing:
Hi, I'm Bridget the midget-brain!
The foxy bar manager waves each away
in a tone that takes stock of their relative
charms: 'Don't tempt me, sweetheart!' 'Ask me
tomorrow.' 'Fuck off, Simon, you gobshite . . .'
and sundry variations. Shortly
from under the waterfront palm trees
a zippy flotilla of tenders discharges,
conveying the revellers to their floating
digs which rock together gently, lit up

like a matchstick city. Ahead lie
the customary late-night bouts of skinny-
dipping and haute cuisine, ruinous card games,
beer and narcotics, and creepy, athletic
rich-person sex. Bridget meanwhile
squares off the tills, locks the night's take in
the wall-safe and closes up behind her.

If the island's south is the muddy side,
the murky side, the shady side,
the burned-out hippie white trash hillbilly
methadone-maintenance P-lab side, then
the landing the locals call Shady Grove
is Southside Central. The South Pole.
So here is another of the island's mysteries.
The slack-timbered houseboats
moored in the mangroves are home to a population
of nine. The patriarch, Groober, and
Cooch (his 'old lady'), come with three
interchangeable, rat-tailed progeny:
Marley, Cassidy and Quinn . There's Leo
the Crab Man. There's Bung-Eye Ben, famed
for his toxic agave liquor. Homebake,
Bung-Eye's singing dog, makes eight.
And then there's Bridget O'Dwyer.
Now, why would the sharpest young woman
on the island – classiest, cutest, most demonstrably
hip – choose to be living on a hairy
old houseboat with a posse of gap-toothed
degenerates? What's *that* about? And yet
somehow nobody likes to ask; it isn't like
Manfred – his eyesight, his money. In Bridget's

case there's a curious chivalry, some obscure
deference owing to her beauty – or owing
(is it this?) to her woundedness. Regardless,
the island accepts it. 'It is what it is.'

Now, as she drives home over the causeway,
she rolls down the windows to drink in
the breeze: the smell of the mudflats, of seagrass
and cockles, ti-tree and diesel and garbage
and cabbage trees in bloom. Why does it
claim her, this skanky old swamp, with its
muddy life scuttling and gurgling
and farting? And why does she put up with
Shady Grove, with the damp, with the rot,
with the paddlecrab gumbo? The swamp people,
quite rightly, think she's a goddess, they want
to protect her, and that's okay. And Bridget?
Well, she's sentimental, too – she knows her
own limits, is how she'd describe it – and
that makes her easy to get alongside
of, and almost impossible to reach.

⋌

Juanita Díaz at her escritoire
has a view of the mainland, the lights of
the city. She can make out the hoopla
of the Klondike Casino, the tacky
little tower thing on top with its lolly-pink
knob. Poker Face is what Joe likes to call her:
an analytic mask without peer in this
poker-faced business. But she isn't

a gambler. And she doesn't like to feel
as if she's being *forced* to gamble. This
character, Frank. Three months and counting,
daily sessions four days a week, and still
she doesn't know what his game is –
only that there is one. *Charm alert*
is what Luis used to say, but
the charmers are easy: Narcissism 101.
It's the client who wants to give it one
more twist, who knows when to *turn it off* –
that's when you've got a player. Who are you,
Mr New Patient Frank? Tell me you're just
an obsessional moper: Papa with his
hacksaw, minor perversions, self-regard so
deeply occulted you truly believe you
don't like yourself. *That* we can work with.
The job gets so lonely when there's no one to
talk to; she'd just like to offload to someone,
a second pair of ears. But even Luis
couldn't help with the first one, back in
BA, at the Escuela Freudiana, that
slimeball sociopath, the professional
footballer. Broke his wife's arm in the car
door – her humerus, he had to point out,
when he came to his session next morning
all pumped up to tell her about it.

In the back of the fridge there's a fifth
of vodka. Briefly her mind creeps
towards it, then tip-toes away again.
We have to keep loving them. That's all we've got.
(Luis, as she lay crumpled up on his couch,

her entire body throbbing with fury that felt
like grief.) And this, she sees now, is where you
learn what that means, adrift at the bottom
of the South Pacific – when you strip out
the language and the coy ceremonials,
the masters, the schools, all the childish
court politics – that's what you're left with:
'a cure through love'. She lets down
the roman blind and takes half an Ambien.

And Manfred Singleton? No sleep for him –
not yet. His sleep demands premeditation.
Manfred's dreams are a single dream, with as
many variations as there are nights
to dream it. He dreams of the mountains he
grew up beneath in a storied homeland
far to the south, of saw-toothed granite
and wind-polished ice, of snow like enamel,
of rivers like burnished wire. He dreams
of a universe ravished of people,
and of all the ten-thousand-odd ways to say
lonely in an atavistic, self-devised language
that no one else speaks. These are the dreams
that by day, at the keyboard, he sculpts into
incomprehensible sounds. They are not
to be rushed, or stumbled into; they
are what he has to show for a lifetime
of lascivious perfectionism. And so
his waking hours wind up by careful degrees.
First, the mix-down of the evening's work;

second, the dusting of all wooden
surfaces; third, the rolling of a modest
joint of blue-ribbon skunk laced with
opium paste; fourth, the leisurely
smoking of same; fifth, ablutions and
asanas; sixth, massage of scalp and temples;
seventh, repair to listening station;
eighth, rotation of remote control eleven
times in each direction; ninth, disinfection
of headphones with antiseptic tissue. And now
our fastidious feral composer, our
oneiric doodler, is ready to push PLAY . . .

The passage of time has become confused.
The playback has ended. Did Manfred
listen? And why is he perched with his chin
on the windowsill, galvanised like a
gundog on point? The inlet below, where some
several hours earlier Marigold's light
caught his vigilant eye, is restored
at this hour to its native gloom, to
the colour that the poet once christened
'bible-black'. A blackout as deep as a starless
sky, across which he finds himself tracking
a smear of light. A comet, it might be,
if this *were* the sky, a reticent smudge
like a match-head just failing to strike.
Phosphorescence, it can only be – but
stirred into life *by what*, exactly? To
interrupt his nightly office – the reader
will gather – is no small thing. But the fallen
heavenly body intrigues him. He must

have his goggles, he must now confirm, in their
washed-out televisual glare, that what he
has been tracking is a human person,
crawling, with a long, steady stroke, in
the direction of shore. *But who? And from
where, at this unlikely hour?* Is Manfred
Singleton paranoid? Let's say, at least,
that he's a symbolic thinker, and that
it's not every day such an odd fowl
swims into his ken. For now the athlete
has gained the shallows, his toes have discovered
the welcome sand where he hauls himself
upright, a turkey-necked Venus,
some two metres tall and stark bollocky
nude! Lurching ashore, in a great
froth of foam, he throws himself down
on the gravel, splayed out like a starfish.
Manfred turns from the window, shaking
his head. Whoever he is, this emissary from
the deep, this portent, this singular bird, he is
here for a reason, Manfred confides, to himself
and to us. We have not seen the last of him.

CHAPTER 2

You never know what you're going to find
on a morning stroll through paradise.
Marigold takes up a bucket of pig food
and picks her way down through the garden in
the rising heat. Lately, rainbow lorikeets
have been coming each morning to the blossoming
flax – interlopers, the purists tell her,
but honestly, can you have too much
colour? Who's going to quarrel with
this, for example: a cock pheasant
scratching between the corn rows, scarlet-
complexioned, horny-wattled, dauntless
in his sumptuary splendour? True, her
morning began with a smoke. Her outlook
is, let's say, *susceptible*. That a kererū
plumped in a loquat tree should fix her
with its pink-rimmed eye and allow
her to pass within touching distance is
not necessarily a sign from the gods.
And yet – as her boys now come blundering
out of the underbrush with their happy cries,
scrummaging one another out of the way

in the fight for their share of her scratches
and smooches – isn't there something (she finds
herself wondering) slightly off-key in
their over-excitement? 'What's up with
you lot, then?' she demands, as the biggest
and bossiest paws at her gumboot,
heavily, with a stubby white trotter –
'Fuck you, buster!' she mutters, as she spanks
his fat arse. That's when she spies, in the trampled
mud by the drinking trough, the tell-tale
pug. A big-footed someone has been here
to drink. Someone who isn't a Berkshire hog!

Below the pig run, her mother's garden
falls through a sequence of landings till it
ends at the beach. Here, above the high-tide
mark, screened by a crumpled pōhutukawa
(just now embarked on its sanguinary
shtick as the barbecue season lights up
the gulf), is the place she assembles her
beachcomber mulch, a pungent confection
of pig straw and fish-frames and kelp.
It's simpler to keep this away from the house;
its charms can be lost on visitors. But
not, she observes, on the author of last
night's mysterious footprint – for here she
discovers him: smeared from groin to
Adam's apple with chocolatey nutritious filth,
a scrawny, suntanned child of Nature,
tossing the stinky midden with a driftwood
crutch! And apparently not discomposed
to be happened upon like this in his

sky-clad trespasses. Exuberantly
he throws down his weapon and thrusts out
in greeting a grungy paw. 'Bardruin!'
he announces, affably. 'Bardruin, Arthur.
You'll have to forgive me, my dear, but
it's truly the most splendid compost –
you know how it is – I just couldn't resist!'

⚔

A scruffy green parrot with a powder-blue
face is perched on a ladderback chair
in Marigold's kitchen. Chuck is his name
(or, more formally, Chuckles – somewhat
misleadingly, given his temperament).
'Chaddie's back! Chaddie's back!' the moth-eaten
creature announces, obscurely. '¿Dónde está
tu ropa, cabrón?' 'Chuck, don't be rude!
Ignore him, he's like this with visitors.'
Briefly, Marigold explains: how the bird
first belonged to her analyst friend;
how he'd gatecrash her sessions, then
share – 'You mean parrot?' – 'Exactly!
Our Chuck's an inveterate gossip. You can
picture the scandal. So he needed a home.'
'I'm guessing your Freudian friend must be
Spanish?' 'Almost. Juanita's from Buenos
Aires. You miss her, don't you, darling boy?
You want to go back to your Mami and all
that talk about fucking.' When her huffy
companion disdains to reply she attempts to
cajole him with peanuts and kisses. The bird,

though, is not to be bought off so cheaply.
'¡Chupa mi pinga!' he irritably croaks.

⚔

When the castaway has been fed and watered,
showered, shaved and acclimatised – his
matted locks trimmed, a bathrobe proffered,
his outlandish, bony dimensions recorded –
his rescuer embarks on her afternoon errands.
'You two boys get to know one another.
I'll be back to make dinner. You never
know – we may have Arthur dressed for it.'

And so, as events transpire, they will. For
St Vincent de Paul has the very thing:
baggy old cords, a grey cotton shirt, even
a Harris tweed jacket. 'For my nephew,'
she explains.
            Before that, however, there's
a stop to be made at an unassuming
weatherboard home just this side of the causeway.
Marigold finds June Te Patu in the shade
of the villa's back porch at her fly-tying
vice. 'Hey, that's a banger!' she rightly
observes of a psychedelic, shrimp-like
confection receiving a last dab of
lacquer. The old lady beams. After
kisses and cuddles, Marigold puts on
the kettle and unwraps her offerings.
'I've made up that kawakawa ointment,
e kui.' 'Did you do it like I told you?'

'Of course I did.' There's a comfrey paste
and rosehip oil, and a freshly caught
snapper ('Look, it's a beauty!'). 'You're
good to us, child. Ae, Koro will love it.'
She slides the fish onto a baking tray.
 'You're good to us, child, but' – *here we go*,
it's a game they've played a hundred times –
'what you need is a man to look after.'
'Auntie, shush!' 'Don't shush me, girl, it's true!
Now what did you do with that fellah, used
to stay up by you – the airline pilot –
what was his name again?' 'Carlos, Auntie.'
'Carlos! That was a nice-looking boy. Auē!
You young people, you don't know what's good for you!'
'Auntie June, I'm fifty-one.' 'Nonsense!'
Marigold strokes her hand. 'Anyway, Auntie,
it wasn't my fault. I liked him, truly,
I did, but then he just . . . disappeared.'

                              ⚹

Marigold, Bardruin swiftly discovers,
is not averse to Life's Good Things. First up,
garfish, dusted in flour and fried to a golden
nicety, pearlescent flesh unzipping
with a sigh, flinty Italian white
mouth-puckeringly dry; the artichoke
and red pepper soufflé arrives with
a crumpety local chardonnay, the compote
of wild mushrooms with a barnyard burgundy.
For one who has lived for the past several
months on a diet of oysters and wild spinach –

but they'll get to that soon enough . . .
Meanwhile his hostess has swept up an
expertly cantilevered armload of
dishes and dead soldiers, departing for
the kitchen, whence, a few moments later,
she emerges with an artful *plateau
de fromages*. They slump in companionable
lassitude, mopping up the pinot.
The silence between them is interrupted
only by incoherent avian
scolding, and the cracking of pistachios.

Finally Marigold calls them to order.
'It's not compulsory,' she says, half-
truthfully, 'no one need sing for his supper,
but . . .' – with a pause, just a hint of theatre –
'. . . I do have a token from a grateful
client laid by for just such a moment
as this. And if you'll forgive me, my
waterlogged friend, it strikes me you're
not one to shy from a drink.' A Baron de
Lustrac Armagnac, honeyed of hue and of
unfathomable age, brings Bardruin
out in a boyish grin. The cork is consigned
to the fireplace. And so he begins . . .

Marigold, may he safely assume, is not
a consumer of poetry? In which case
she is perhaps unaware of the scandal that
lately, in certain small circles, has attached to
the Bardruin name: to wit, his naming,
shaming and slating for re-education

by the Continence Police. No?
His hostess looks amiably blank.

'The story is long more than edifying.
I am, you will gather, a maker of
verses. In the Age of Universal
Enjoyments (which you, I suspect, are too
young to remember) I entertained briefly
a modest fame. Celebrant of the happy urge,
I wrote, I declaimed my works in public,
I was even received in the precincts
of higher learning. Girls would come out in
their long summer dresses, smoking, pressing
flowers in their notebooks, attending
gravely as I teased apart the great
perplexities of the day. There were problems,
you see, and we fully meant to solve them:
the problem of leisure, the politics of Joy,
the toxic cathode, the Militant
Orgasm. My poems were like drugs. Like
explosives! Like radios!! Ah, well . . .'

The part that comes next demands a three-finger
refill. History takes its pound of flesh:
the Age of Austerity, the first Great
Divestment, the rise of the Excellence
Party, the Commission for Outputs.
'Remember the first talk of private prisons?
Lord how we laughed. *It will never work!*
What would be next, we asked, private
police? We all should have bought shares in
Punishment Corp. *Haaarrgh!*' There's a clatter

of indignant birdlife as poor Chuckles scatters
his shells in alarm, then hops from the table
to his mistress's shoulder to be petted
and soothed. ('Just war stories, darling.')
The Shouting Man stares with reflective
mien, as if waiting for the narrative
to clear in his brandy balloon.

'The motherfucking Salvation Army, how's
that for a joke? All that real estate standing
idle, the hospitals, the drying-out centres . . .
the bean-counters dream up Citizen Law
and next thing you know we've got the Gulag
Archipelago! Salvation Redux
– a refit for every new crime!
There's all these brand new consortia, right,
then the Poetry Instructors get in
on the act: the PIs, the Sallies, the Culture
Bureau, Punishment Corp. Well, here I am . . .'

'What you seem to be telling us,' Marigold
offers, ever attentive, repairing
their drinks, 'what you seem to be saying is
you're a fugitive.'
                    'What I seem to be
saying, my dear, is that I'm dead! Listen . . .

'A year ago as a birthday treat (a round
number, please don't ask!) my publisher,
bless him, let me have a *New and Selected*.
My star, as I've said, was a little tarnished,
I'd not been exactly in the public eye.

Well, I got some attention all right – it was
just the wrong kind! They hauled me in
front of the Continence Board. When they find
you in breach they give you a choice: you can
either recant – you hand in your card, you
grovel, you promise not to publish again –
or they ship you out for re-education.
They gave me a week to decide . . .'

⤢

Proceedings by now have become rather loose.

When Marigold comes to, the following morning,
the sky bright, Bardruin cast up beside her,
she will find that the Baron has gone to
his grave and taken with him all but scattered
fragments of the tale's remaining stanza.
A drowning was staged, she remembers that,
and an exit contrived in a dinghy
to an offshore islet . . . a menu of shellfish
and dried beef jerky in the course of a
month or two outstayed its welcome . . . something,
too, about the loss of the transport, floating
away on a spring flood, the decision
to swim which, as tide flows would have it,
brought the trouserless poet to Marigold's
shore. A poet no longer entirely
resigned – this much she recalls quite plainly,
accompanied as the announcement was
by antic dance moves, chest percussion
and vehemence enough to send a startled parrot

fluttering roofwards in fear of his life:

*Fuck those sanctimonious fucking class
monitors – Bardruin isn't finished yet!*

CHAPTER 3

Every Friday tricky Frank Hortune
joins the commuters on the early boat,
catches the train to a well-to-do suburb out
west of the city, drinks three cups of coffee,
and finally, when he can delay no
longer, makes the twenty-minute walk
up the hill to the retirement facility.
Where his mother is dying of . . . *what*,
exactly? Frank can never fully explain.
The tremors are merely the part you can
see; some kind of internal bleeding is
doing the real damage.
　　　　　　　'Internal bleeding –
that's a colourful phrase,' says Juanita.
'Internal to whom, do you think?'
　　　　　　　　　　　Weakly,
and though he knows better, Frank laughs.
'Boundaries . . . really? How long do we have?'

The analyst has all the time in the world.
To pass it, she steeples her fingertips.

'Did I say that she still has her cello in there?
It's fifteen years, at least, since she played –
the Parkinson's – but she keeps it with her,
propped in the corner. Like Bentham's corpse!
God knows why: it used to make her
unhappy enough even when she was well.
She hadn't performed since ages back –
she'd play for her students, that was all –
but we knew how it pained her, she made sure
of that. And I was supposed to learn, of course.
She pushed it, I think. I was still too
young, too small, I could barely get round
the neck; but it wasn't that – it was too much
demand; the intensity, it choked me up . . .'

A pause. He hears footsteps: Christian
Bogdanovic, crunching outside down
the shell path, en route to his writing class.

'In the end we made a deal: if I switched to
piano she'd let me off. So I found
my own teacher – a man, middle-aged, he
was strict, but I liked him – and, well, that
was it. No one had to make me practise.
I knew right away, I just grabbed it, and ran.
Of course Mum then decided that we had
to play duets. Christ, if I never hear
the Moonlight fucking Sonata again
it'll be too soon! And my father would
sit there pretending to listen with this
crafty satirical look on his face . . .'

'The magistrate? He was no judge of music.'

'He was no judge of anything much, at home.
He put on his slippers and left her to it.
Mind you, after he died it was worse . . .'

'Of course. There was no one to stop the bleeding,
the deal was off. No wonder you ran.'

＜

Christian Bogdanovic, poet, critic and
deputised agent of the Continence Police,
inclines to a short-sleeved, preppy demeanour
and a firmly old-school pedagogy.
Phones in a bucket. *Rap tap tap*
goes the rattan cane on the whiteboard.
Rap tap tap. In the open-air fale with
its dress circle view a dozen anxious
supplicants crouch at their desks. The gulf
steps away in seraphic blues. A fizzboat
leaves a wake like a smear of spittle.

But right now every eye is on Mei-Lin
Chin. The soles of Christian's John Lobb deck shoes
creak as he paces. The young woman reads:

> *The eye is an otter.*
> *The body is water.*
> *The eye has no lover:*
> *its home is the river.*

Palely on the reedy verge
the otter catches forty winks.

And poetry?
The eye clouds over.
It fails to see what les autres
are getting so worked up about.

Arrested, like a stalking heron, bayonet
drawn above a tidal pool, the instructor
peers out at the scenery. Nobody breathes . . .

Well? He rounds on his nervous flock:
Somebody? Anybody? What do we think?

The question is strictly rhetorical,
of course; no one is foolish enough to
respond – although Ms Chin, it turns out,
has done rather well; in her text we can hear
many voices, not unlike the river.
The room lets go of its collective breath.
Once more Christian's boat shoes begin to squeak.

✄

'The curious thing is I look at that cello
and I want to pick it up and play it.
It's a gorgeous instrument – Johannes Brückner,
1920s – it needs to be played. Not
by me, I hasten to add! And I don't . . .
I mean, *really*, I don't want to play it,
I just want to pick it up, hold it . . .'

'So: do you, or don't you?'

'What?'

'Want to play.'

'No! Maybe. I don't know . . . I can't, I can't even
touch it.'

'Why?'

'Why? It would be like touching *her*.'

'Which you can't.'

'There isn't a chance in hell.
It's as if there's a force-field around her.
I can't reach through it.'

'It's puzzling, though, don't
you think, that force? I mean: this is your
forte, with women, you know how to touch them.'

Less than a compliment, Frank understands.
Even so, he struggles not to sound too pleased.

'It's interesting to watch the staff. They
made such a fuss when she first came in.
Your mother, they'd tell me, she's such a
strong person, we so enjoy having her . . .
all that shit – that *stuff*, okay – they're great, they
mean it – but I'm not hearing nearly so
much of it now. It isn't *just me* is what
I'm trying to say. They've begun to get
a sense of what they're up against, how
hard she is to care for. These days
they're more sympathetic towards me . . .'

'These staff who – let me guess – are women?
And who are touched. Who find Frank touching.'

36

'You – yes, you – I've forgotten your name . . .'
'It's William Chang, sir.' 'Read to us, Chang.'

The dawn that breaks on your small estate:
its ardour, as if it would punish the eyes,
while the stumbling bee alights on the trembling –

'Stop! For Christ's sake *stop!*' THWACK!!
The cane strikes the desk with a sickening slurp.
Highlighter pencils leap like startled game.
'On your feet!' And the miserable youth,
arraigned by an earlobe, is marched to the front.

'Tell me, Mr Trembling Blossom, do you
find it amusing to make us all puke?
There, look' – again, the instructional
yank on the ear to direct the gaze – 'what
is the name of that island, my febrile friend?'

On the distant horizon, a blue shape
hovers, a white puff of smoke at its cone
like a thought balloon. 'The Isle of Drunks, Sir?'
'*The Isle of Drunks!* Indeed. And what do you think
happens there?' When the boy fails to answer
('*Speak! We can't hear you!*') his classmates press
forward to peck at the corpse. 'Please sir,
Prison, sir.' 'Re-education sir!' 'Sobering
up, sir?' '*You hear that, boy?* And this goes for
everyone. *Write this down!* If anyone wants
to get through this course, then spare us your

dramas, spare us your feelings and *spare us*
your wretched qualifiers! Do I make myself clear?
Chang, back to your seat. Now, all of you' –
a brief caesura, every eye fixed on the moving
finger – 'all of you have forty-five minutes.'
Rap tap tap. 'Sestinas. Repeat after me . . .'
Inscribed in irascible caps on the whiteboard,
the classroom discerns its laborious fate.

SUFFERING
TESTIFY
SHOPPING LIST
PATHOS
FRUITINESS
SNIVELLING

'What are you waiting for?
These things aren't going to write themselves!
Nobody leaves this room till they're all on my desk.'

Juanita is nothing if not High Church:
the couch with its iconic Persian rug,
the therapist stationed behind it, analysis
a tergo. At the patient's feet stands
a narrow bookshelf – a modest thing, given
its onerous cargo: Sade and Joyce, Bataille
and Borges, Lautréamont, Lorca, Mallarmé,
Proust – solemn reminder of why we're here,
but a lure for the wandering eye, the drifting . . .
Whoah! Through the wall comes a startling slap.

'A Child Is Being Beaten,' Frank observes,
nimbly. Now it's Juanita's turn to laugh; she
grants him a moment to enjoy his small victory –
time for the ripples to sink, and settle – then
summons them back to their responsibilities.

'Your mother retired from the concert stage,
you said. But I'm not sure precisely when.'

'Oh, that. The sixty-four-dollar question.'
'Costly.'
              'She wouldn't exactly say.'

                                    'Or costive?'
'Yes, of course. That too. But like I said, the mail
gets through: there's always bloody old Jeremy
Bentham glowering at me from the corner –
I've always known. *You're so damned lucky* – no,
that's not right, so "jolly" lucky, is what she'd
say – *you're so jolly lucky being able to play
and you don't even bother.* God, how
many times . . . ? So yes, okay, the career
died in childbirth – there, I've said it.
But all the same . . . I got to know this
violinist, Grete her name was –
a refugee, or her parents were, she'd
arrived as a child at the start of the war –
and she'd played with her. In a string quartet,
which was Mum's big thing. I didn't press,
I don't know why, you'd think I'd want to
find out, right? Finally, though, what Grete
said was – literally, her very words – *your
mother's playing was a little bit cold.*

I know – I shouldn't laugh, but hell, the cello
of all things! She had no *feel*. And I think my
father knew this too. Or is that too kind . . . ?'

'Too *kind*, you say.' And when Frank doesn't
answer: 'So . . . the dead career was a beat-up?'

'That's what I'm wondering. The Old Man,
you see, he wasn't a philistine, nothing
like that. But he never went along with
that story, the whole Maria Callas thing.'

'Your father, you're saying, was not a team player.
Perhaps a bit *callous*.'
                                    'Is that what you hear?'

'And yet not such a hard player, not with his son.
I don't hear the child being beaten by his father.'

CHAPTER 4

The low-slung, rust-emblazoned barn that
is Wiremu Te Patu's General Store
sits at the junction on the northeast ridge
where the dry-weather road turns off to Barnacle
Bay. Whatever you can't find at Koro Bill's
you can safely assume you won't need on the island.
Fancy a crack at the bad-tempered reef break
that gives the bay its modest fame? Bill can put
you on a V3 Rocket or a second-hand Jon Pyzel.
Can't find the right brand of nước màu sauce
to marinate those broadbill steaks? The requirements
of Thai, Malaysian and Vietnamese cuisines
are more than catered for. It's all here
somewhere: from handcrafts to handcuffs, from
boat shoes to brake shoes, from big game
tackle to Hippie Hannah's notorious bath
salts and headshop gee-gaws.
                        'Morning, luv,'
says Marigold, to a straw-haired, starved-
looking woman in a cavernous greatcoat.
Her cheerfulness earns her an uncertain smile
from a face that must once have been handsome

but has long since lost its architecture.
Another time she might try harder, but
today she too is on an urgent mission –
and not, for once, in the liquor or fishing gear
aisles. Leaving the other to her contemplation
of Hannah's ornamental glassware, she edges
past and pushes on into the labyrinth.

Koro Bill looks up from his crossword,
shelving his pencil behind his ear.
(*Temptress comes of losing lover's head in
orbit. Five letters.*) 'Tēnā koe, e Koro,'
the customer croaks, as she shuffles to
the counter. 'Morning, Cooch.' From her basket
she unloads a loaf of bread, an iceberg
lettuce (which Koro wraps), a small tin
of cat food, pineapple Tim Tams, a $2 packet
of live bait balloons. 'And the meth pipe, e whaea?
Are you paying for that?' From her coat
she surrenders the punctured flask. 'Of course
I am, Koro.' She is not, she reminds him,
a morning person. (She can say *that* again.)

⤫

The store is like the village pump:
sooner or later you catch up with everyone.
If they're not here to shop, it's to hang out
and gossip, to smoke weed and strum ukuleles,
to play petanque in the parking lot.
Juan and Conchita sell empanadas and coffee
out of a fifties caravan. Hipsters pretend to be

tightrope walkers and generally 'make sport' for
their neighbours. Olive enthusiasts
pretend to be farmers, propping themselves
against dusty utilities, grousing,
wrinkling their crows' feet, masticating grass.

Speaking of wankers, here's Simon Richwhite,
shopping for a new intake grate for his jet ski.
His gargantuan SUV pulls up
in a shower of gravel. He flounces inside,
flipping a hang loose salute at Conchita
who mirrors the gesture with mirthless
solemnity. Meanwhile she's frothing
the almond milk for two decaf lattes
for Justin and Harriet, Christian's offsiders
from the poetry school who drop by the store
every Friday for the latest *LRB*.
Justin's rummaging through it now while Harriet
stretches her quads and hammies. She's been
known to show up for class in her bike shorts.
The island is something you get, or you don't.

⚔

In the shade of a suitably aged magnolia, four
veteran bikers take their ease. Big Wayne,
Little Wayne, Shane and Zane: known to one and all
as the Zimmermen. The soubriquet (think:
'assisted mobility') is not altogether
kindly meant, but what do these badass
hombres care as they blat round the village
four-abreast on their motorised golf buggies?

With a ghetto blaster the size of a fridge
they terrorise young folk the island over,
ho-ho-hoing, talking shit, and straining their
thermos coffee through grizzled moustachios.

Zane has a joke that he never tires of. 'Yo,
Justin!' he bellows – being deaf – 'did I
tell you about the time I met Charles Bukowski?'
He laughs till he splutters, while Justin looks up
with a puzzled, nothing-to-see-here expression
which might or might not be designed to conceal
the fact that he has no idea what's so funny.
'Justin, what are you reading, brother?' But
the young man is already far away, immersed
in a testy review of the latest James Fenton.

✐

'I know it's here somewhere,' says Koro Bill
from the top of a ladder. 'Ah, here we go!'
Marigold reaches up for the bundle.
She carries it back to the counter where
she folds back the oilcloth. 'Goodness
me!' And indeed it's a beauty, an object of
solemn equipoise: the Bakelite housing
is boot-burnish black, the keys are a
gridwork of floating planets, concave,
as if they've been worn away by the endless
attentions of fingertips. Their functions
are spelled out in inlaid brass of the same
sober hue as the proper name: SMITH CORONA.
The storekeeper slaps down a ream of paper,

rolls a crisp sheet onto the drum. Marigold
puts the quick brown fox through its paces:
the keys fall with measured rectitude. 'May
I?' asks Koro, in his gentlemanly way,
scrunching back the sleeves of his smock.

> *Like a Poet hidden*
> *In the light of thought,*
> *Singing hymns unbidden*

he types, then rolls up for inspection. The ink
is black, the impress even, the handsomely
serifed font stands out present and correct.
'I could sell you a laptop more cheaply, of course . . .'
'But why would I want that?' 'Why indeed?'
The carriage return rings tunefully
as he strokes the gravely weighted keys:

> *The sub-sheriff Long John Fanning appears,*
> *smoking a pungent Henry Clay.*
> *But that is another pair of trousers.*
> *Which side is your knowledge bump?*

⚹

Had Conchita not chosen this of all
mornings to offer up a something-less-than-
scalding-hot latte . . . had Marigold just
done as Koro suggested and taken home
the typewriter wrapped in its cover . . . but
no, the unhappy events must be told:
how, while Harriet – having explained succinctly

her expectation of appropriate service –
waits for the icily polite barista
to (quote) *do better next time*, Marigold,
arms weighed down with her bargain, takes her
leave, backwards, through the flystrip curtain,
turning in time to avoid (by a whisker!)
a headbutt collision with the glowering young woman.
In hideous stop-time Marigold sees it:
the breathless, blazing December day,
the trilling cicadas, the ice-cream wrappers,
Koro's dog in his accustomed shade; and
her own triumphant – then mortified – look
as Justin starts up from his *LRB* while
his co-worker's frankly inquiring gaze
tracks from her face to her cargo and
neutrally back again. *Something isn't right
with this picture.* More than this Harriet
couldn't explain, but it hangs like an
incomplete sentence, an unresolved chord.
Marigold, meanwhile, recovers her poise –
'Buenos días, Conchita darling!' – and yet,
all the way to her shabby old truck, she can feel,
boring into her shoulder blades, Harriet's stare.

CHAPTER 5

The Farmhouse kitchen, a business meeting.
Present: Sigrid, Juanita and Joe.
Agenda: promotional activities (in attendance,
Bridget O'Dwyer), WWOOFers and – call it
'general business' – the customary
fulminations of ex-professor Bravo.

⚔

The annual shindig has long outgrown
the news-grabbing function that initially
gave rise to it. These days it's more a kind
of feudal largesse: a calendar fixture,
the party of the island summer. Yet
more than this, as her partners intuit –
though neither would be quite so mean as to
say – the Ball is Sigrid's private trip,
a once-a-year dalliance in showbiz,
her chance to play Doctor Goodvibes.
Bridget checks in on behalf of the venue:
menu, security, ticketing, disabled access.
She also feeds Sigrid her favourite question:

'How's the band coming together?' Well,
funny you should ask. For just now she's come
from her ritual briefing with guitar-ace
Groober and his unlikely sidekick (whose
hand she had held and whose hormones
titrated through a lifetime of startling
refashionings – *viz*. Manfred Singleton).
Once a year a pick-up band is dreamed up
out of their two strange heads, and once
a year the rafters shake, the beer jugs fly
and the Sandgroper generally goes off.
'And the ring-in?' Bridget wants to know.
'What was his name again . . . Hank?' 'Frank.
Quite the talent, according to Groober.
Dr Díaz here needs to be nice to him.'
Bridget, gathering her phone and keys,
exchanges a sidelong glance with her friend.
'Adiós,' she tells the room
pleasantly. 'Play nicely, everyone.'

⟆

WWOOFers: a sore point, always has been.
No one remembers how the idea took hold.
Sigrid likes to mother the young; Joe (he
can hardly deny it) is happy just to
look at them. But so, too, he points out,
and with good cause, are the prosperous
late middle-lifers who keep the show solvent;
what are they dreaming of, after all, if
not fluffy white bathrobes and pony-
tailed Scandinavians ferrying smart drinks?

They intern, then, for bed and board: the budding
Ayurvedists and Lymphatic Drainers,
the apprentice Body Harmonists, the Core
Energeticists. All summer long they
wash up at the door with their backpacks and their
grubby sarongs, and the sea breeze grows sweet
with their youth and their accented English.
And yes, perhaps they keep the place fresh. But
the Farm's reputation? It's a delicate thing.
Sigrid – let's not forget this – is a doctor:
her rationalism is bred in the bone;
she knows there are more things in heaven
and earth, etc., but, seriously, Myofascial
Release Massage? Thought-field therapy?
And let's not get started on last summer's
menace, 'Dr' Candida (Candy) Sweetmeadow,
masseuse, astrologer, self-described Reichian
life coach (translation: *Sausalito beach-tramp*)
who set out to 'treat' every man on the island,
not excluding the ex-professor. So
there are, shall we say, certain undercurrents
directing the conversation off-course – and yet
always it beaches in exactly the same place:
'Yes,' Joe agrees, 'we should tighten up. So
what about the Three-Headed Monster?'
He means, of course, the creative writers,
Justin, Christian and Harriet. The Terrible
Triplets. 'For heaven's sake,' he's saying now, for
what feels like the hundredth time, 'how is anyone
meant to get "well" with those three strutting
about the place like God's gift to Rectitude?'

Juanita, who has heard all this often enough
to know how it ends, takes her leave of the meeting.
'You may not admire them, long-suffering
spouse, but –' *'You've just got the hots for Harriet!'*
'Fuck you, mister! That's unfair!' 'I withdraw
and apologise . . .' 'As I was saying – have you
any idea what your average well-heeled doting
parent is willing to pay to see their child
certificated in the genteel art of composition?'
'. . .' 'And what would you say was the total net
income last year from your study group on Northrop
Frye?' 'Perhaps I need to promote it harder.'
'That's one solution. But meanwhile, Jonah,
until we find a better way of paying
your liquor bill . . .' 'Yes. Very well. It shall be
as you say.' As it usually is. The writers stay.

Wanda Blissball, zipping her gym bag, blows
out the candles and exits her studio.
Warm night air comes to greet her like a big
friendly dog. She climbs by a path of crushed
white shell; in her ears are the stridulant
buzz-saws of crickets, in her nostrils
the scent of gardenias and night-blooming
jimson. But Wanda's awareness is all
in her spine – the which, for the last ninety
minutes, has been lavishly exercised.
The session began with some gentle salutes,
Adho Mukha Vrksasana, Setu Bandha,
exploratory Pigeon; then working her

50

way up through Locust and Camel into
Urdhva Dhanurasana, King Cobra and
Rajakapotasana. On the distant
horizon, Vrischikasana, the Scorpion . . .
not in this lifetime, perhaps? Never mind.
As Wanda will tell you, she's 'all about
the journey' – not to mention soused
with adrenaline and creamy endorphins.

The path to her sleep-out leads past the digs
of her recent acquaintance Frank Hortune,
Juanita's new client. Frank's on the porch
of his chalet with a parlour guitar. 'Evening
Miss Wanda.' He leaves off his picking, touches
his hat-brim sardonically. 'Care for a toot?'
'Thank you, no, I'm nicely done. But I'll
visit a while if you'll play something. Don't
mind me . . .' He doesn't. (Cue vigorous bubbling
of bongwater.) He breathes out an expansive cloud.
'Sure I can't tempt you?' 'Truly, I'm good.
I've just come from backbending.' 'Ah, I see.'
'Tell me, though – I'm curious – what does
your analyst say about this? I mean, your
getting high and all.' Frank sits a moment
in something like thought; he fingers an absent-
minded chord. 'It's funny. She's got this
high-priestess thing going on, but she's not
the prohibitive type. You have to remember,
it's all very French – surrealist, you know?
The badder the better. Don't be obvious,
don't be dull, don't give up on your own
desire. Otherwise it's no holds barred.'

'The hell? I thought this was therapy.'
'*Mais non, ma chère. C'est la psychanalyse.*
She tells me I'm bound up inside my language,
she wants to get in there and cut me free' – 'You're
whacked!' – 'with the sharpened edge of the Letter!'
'Frank, what on earth are you talking about?'
'Honestly? I've no idea.' Wanda moves on
without hearing her tune, but it's not
like she needs it. Her spine is still singing.

'You seem very quiet tonight. Do
you feel like talking?' No reply.
A shoulder is all that's available so
Juanita kisses it. 'Today was my birthday,'
says Bridget at last. (*What?*) But she means her
recovery birthday, her anniversary, she's
seven years clean. 'So your friends made a fuss
at the meeting?' 'I wasn't at the meeting.'
'Oh Bridget!' (*No, stop it. Get hold of yourself.*)
'I'm sorry. I just wanted someone to worry.'
'You're worried about your recovery,
aren't you?' 'Juanita, just drop it
for Christ's sake. I'm not your patient.'

Stupid. Where it all went wrong was at work
last night. It was just that song. The Pogues,
on the jukebox – someone kept playing
'A Pair of Brown Eyes'. And that was her dad:
the same old theme-pub Irish shite, the booze,
the sentimental blather. (Triggered –

she hates that word – but it always gets her.)
Once more, then, the dopey saga, spun
the same way every time, as if to a child
who can't stand the smallest thing being changed –
you're telling it wrong! – her dad, his driving,
the singing. And Erin, the whippet.
It wasn't so often, a handful of times,
when things got too busy at her mother's
job, that she'd let her go out on his
road trips. Three or four days. He'd work
the provincial service centres – whatever
it was he was selling at the time – and they'd
put up in motels, but always with long drives
at night. And that was the best bit, the bit she
comes back to, and plays with, and rubs till
it shines like a luminescent road sign:
the cone of the headlights, the dog in her lap,
and the bottle of Redbreast between his
knees – his Irish whiskey, his Irish tenor –
a drunk with a big soppy Irish heart.
The songs that she always forgets she
remembers. The warmth of the sleeping dog,
with her smell, like toast. And it wasn't his
fault – the cow in the low beam, the wagon on its
roof in the hay paddock, engine still running.
*It's all right love, it's all right love, I've
got you.* Tearing his shirt in strips to bandage
her arm – it didn't hurt – there was blood, but
her face wasn't cut, he kept checking and
checking. And not till they'd scrambled
back to the road (he was cradling her head,
they were sitting together while they waited

53

for a vehicle but nothing was coming),
it wasn't till then she remembered: *What
about Erin?* Where had she got to . . . *Dad?
Dad!*

And crying now, the grown-up Bridget,
telling the story in Juanita's bed. 'I can't
tell you how much he loved that dog: it was
something to do with how fragile she was, so
fine-boned and timid. She'd sleep on his pillow.
And now she'd gone out through the windscreen, lost.
I kept saying, "Dad, she'll be scared, go and
find her. You've got to!" He wouldn't. I was
begging him. *Please!* But he just said, "It's all right,
we'll come back tomorrow." He didn't want to
leave me. He stayed. He kept stroking my hair.'

This time Juanita does better, she keeps
her own counsel. Whatever her remit
as analyst-sweetheart, it isn't to
point out the obvious. Not that it's easy.
But Bridget – beneath all the alley-cat glamour –
is so young and prideful, so easily bruised.
Don't touch her stories, she breathes to herself,
that's what her skin's for, you simpleton.
Just touch her skin. And soon enough the girl
is snuffling lightly as she falls asleep.
The cottage, too, its timbers settling. A pipe
that shudders once, then stops. And drifting
from somewhere below in the dark, a guitar
playing just too discreetly to make out the tune.

CHAPTER 6

The poster features a pair of cane toads
copulating in a cocktail glass. ESTRATAB
and the SANDGROPER LOUNGE proudly present,
for one night only – folks, it's the Island's favourite
KNEES-UP, Hop On Down to the HRT
BALL! Prizes! Giveaways! On the bandstand
Frankie Fandango and the Phantasmatics!
♫ ♫ ♫ ♪ ♫ ♫ ♪ ♫ ♫
'Oh!' says Arthur. 'Marigold, please!!'
She can feel it coming off him in waves,
from that deep-down, crumpled-little-boy place
where the terrible disappointments live.
'Darling I'm sorry! You know it's not safe.'
But the dancing, he wails . . .
'Oh, sweetheart! – I won't be too late.'

The Sandgroper, festooned in party lights,
sails through the opalescent dusk.
Sigrid (regal) and Joe (fried and jovial)
edge through the buzzy throng to a stage-side table.

They join a group already well on the way:
a typically mellow and spaced-out Wanda,
and backpacker-intern Willow Durst, abetted
by Marigold and June Te Patu, have seen off
a magnum of Pol Roger. Now Marigold
returns from the bar with a pitcher of margaritas.
'Repeat after me,' announces Joe, as
salt-rimmed glasses are duly charged:
'To the Worried Well.' ('The Worried Well!')
And from Wanda, accepting a refill: 'Namaste!'

There are two empty chairs: Juanita's
and Koro Bill's. Koro by now is behind his kit as
the Phantasmatics noodle through a warm-up set:
cocktail jazz and island chestnuts (a laid-back
synth-driven 'Wipeout', 'Pearly Shells').
Tonight Dr Díaz is happier in the courtyard.
Ever since Gaucho Airways discovered
a cheap way to put up their staff between flights
a cinderblock condo on Palmetto Beach
has been known among locals as the Latin
Quarter. The flight-crews are gone now
(sorry June), but the name and the Latin
connection remains. Young Argentinians,
the odd Chilean – winemakers, fishing
guides, miscellaneous backpackers –
still bring their storybook swagger, their
absurd good looks. Tonight, though, the Quarter
has emptied out, decanted into the Sandgroper
courtyard, where a vast hunk of beef (thank you
Juan and Conchita) caramelises
on a makeshift grill while the señoritas

dance absent-mindedly and the señors
show off at Keepie Uppie. Juanita
they treat with the curious reverence that
the Pampas extends to her solemn craft.
Doctora, they call her, and *Doña Freud*.
Or they tease her with lame but recondite
jokes ('See that slab of meat? Well, it doesn't
see you!'). Sometimes she needs this. They're
only kids, but they *do* see her (that's what
the joke says) and that's what she misses.

Meanwhile the Frankie Fandangos
ease into their work. It all begins with
the rhythm section: alongside Koro, Paulie
Laulala, deckhand by day on the game-fish boats,
an artist with a gaff as no less surely
with a Fender Precision bass. Dreadlocks
bouncing, Paulie probes ahead of the beat while
Koro's kickdrum lollops lazily behind,
as if to say 'Chill, my brother,' and *chill*
is the word. Groober plays his lawsuit era
Ibanez Telecaster copy like someone telling
an elaborate joke, each lick a faked-up
citation from the great Book of Twang.
To the left of the stage, a dimly lit
logjam of turntables, keyboards and audio
doodads conceals the hyperactive form
of Manfred who (goggled, wired off his skull)
scratches, chitters and squeals like an electronic
pack rat. As for the man of the moment, Frank,

he plays the piano as if with his shoulders,
and deals in an affable, rustic tenor
to a catalogue of rockabilly
wig-outs and roadhouse dependables.

The custom here is couple dancing: swing
moves, honky-tonk, old school rock'n'roll.
Pigtails fly in all directions. Modest knickers
flash under cartwheeling skirts. Harriet
dances with Christian, then Justin; Sigrid
with Willow (Wanda being too blissed out).
Cooch does the Shingaling with grumpy Leo
and Lindy Hops gamely with Bung-Eye Ben.
June drags a bashful Joe to his feet
and coaches him in (something like) six count
swing to a thumping rendition of Ike
Turner's 'Rocket 88'. Threads in a
tapestry of cheerful chaos. From the Farm's
cedar chalets come stringy-sinewed
tennis matrons and captains of industry,
caravans and shacks discharge the local
riff raff, and shit-kicking Phantasmatic
grooves shake them all up together.
Seconded for the evening as Bridget's
bar usefuls, Cooch and Groober's feral
progeny scurry underfoot fetching glasses
and stealing unattended drinks. Simon
Richwhite, dressed to impress in his bluest jeans
and blackest shirt, whispers in every available
ear his desire to 'hang out' and snort coke
from off some lucky winner's breastbone.

Supper time. The band quits the stage
as platters of sizzling pampas beef
arrive from the courtyard, crusted with
charred fat and dripping with bloodthirsty
juice-loosening goodness. With flagons of
house red following closely, more than one
wavering vegan is despoiled of his virtue.

In the intermission Sigrid at last gets
her chance to grill Marigold. 'Tell me, darling.
what have you done' – a precautionary
glance, but nobody's listening – 'what have
you done with your bibulous poet? You
know we're all dying to see for ourselves.'
Marigold, mouth full of strip loin, marks time
with her fork . . . 'He's shut up at home tonight with
Chuck; it's difficult, he's a pig-headed cuss,
he's toiling away at some futile poem . . .
You realise it's not *you* I'm hiding him from?'
Again Sigrid glances across at the Triplets,
upright and sober at the neighbouring table.
'Pissheads, eh?' To which, with a sigh
and an *oy vey* shrug, the women drink.

Meanwhile, Sigrid's other half is in deep
conversation with Captain Blood – New
England gentleman, charter boat skipper
and billfish-whisperer extraordinaire.
The Skipper, as it happens, likes to talk
about poetry; the former professor

likes to talk about fishing – a chiastic
roadblock surmounted however by
a problem that neither has ever grown
tired of, the prompt of a thousand
intense disputations: who was the more
skilful angler – Zane Grey or Hemingway?
Is this the occasion on which this intractable
problem might finally be resolved? Alas,
dear reader, we'll never know. Blame Arthur
Bardruin. (Why not? Everyone else does.)

⚔

The first intimation that something's not right
comes when Marigold, pausing in her conflab
with Sigrid, casts her eye towards the stage.
The Phantasmatics are about to kick
off again – Groober noodling, Frank test-testing
on his vocal mic, Koro detuning
his toms – but Manfred, behind his barrage
of keyboards, is staring transfixed at
the back of the room. And it's then, in that
instant before she can turn, as Manfred
locks his gaze on hers, that a voice she would
recognise anywhere, a voice with the timbre of
squealing chalk, penetrates the ambient
chatter:
          Fetch me a Mai Tai, Ping Pong.
                                        'Oh,
fuck!' says she. The two women, turning now
as one, discover a scene even worse
than she feared. Not only have parrot and poet

escaped, but the poet has chosen to
do so unclothed! With Chuck on his shoulder
he leans at the bar rail, torching a grandiose
cigar. Ice-water courses through Marigold's
veins. Tearing off her voluminous poncho
(of her archaic long johns, the less said . . .)
and glancing just once at the table, stage right,
where the Triplets are already on their feet,
she flings herself headlong towards the bar
where she wraps the indignant intruder
in a ball-and-all crush. Sigrid, too, leaps
into action; to Joe she mouths: 'Riot.'
Groober, God love him, deciphers her
semaphore, signals to Paulie, Koro
and Frank, and tears off the anthemic
opening riff of a pleasing – if dubious –
southern rocker. By the time Frank is enthusing
(straight-faced) about being *with his family
once again*, the dance floor is heaving,
beer froth is spraying, and golf carts (4)
are gunning up the disabled access. Sigrid
grabs Willow; each grabs a poetry instructor
and muscles him onto the floor. Harriet
finds her escape route blocked by
(oh God!) the goofy embrace of Joe.
'The pleasure, may I?' he bawls in her ear
as she glares, incredulous, over his shoulder
at Marigold hauling her blanketed
gatecrasher bodily through the swinging glass
doors. Christian, slipping Sigrid's tackle, elbows
his way through the throng in pursuit, only to
crash head-first into a pirouetting golf cart.

A sound erupts that could almost be gunfire
(or might just be Manfred's Minimoog).
Zane bends over his poleaxed victim:
'Everyone get back, give him some air!
Can you hear me, brother? Did I ever tell you
about the time I met Ronnie Van Zant?'

⚔

After a live gig it's always the same:
on the heels of a mild satisfaction,
the soul-skinning clarity. For a pick-up
outfit they weren't at all bad, in places
they even kicked arse and took names;
as Frank says to Paulie, with grooves like that . . .
and the bass player grins like a sunrise.
(Frank means it, too.) But after the first flush
of high fives and back-slapping, after
the shots and the random hugs, as the punters
drift out and the room starts to settle and
the growl of the dishwasher sounds from the bar,
what's left is that question, older than Elvis,
older than Sunday afternoon, the question
that no one should be left alone with.
You mean to say, that's all there is?

Manfred has crated his various toys. Koro
heads out with the last of his kit. Now
nothing remains but an upright piano
(no more than moderately out of tune)
and Frank, with a smoke burning out
in the ashtray, a hint of incipient

tinnitus humming in the background.
Wanda and Willow set the tables to rights,
the small Groobers gather up the broken
crockery, Cooch mops the floor, the last stray
tipplers are swept unprotesting out
into the darkness. Somebody turns
out the house lights.

And then there were three.

If someone (Juanita? Bridget?) were later
to ask for a reason, he couldn't explain.
'The Devil made me do it,' perhaps;
it's probably as good an answer as any.
The issue is, truthfully, can you blame him?
How could anyone – let alone Frank – not
succumb to the moment's ineluctable
theatre? He fingers a lachrymose
minor-key turnaround, thinks better, shifts
it down a tone, and then haltingly, *con
gran tristeza* –

> *Gin makes a woman wanna fight,*
> *then fuck, then cry,* he sings –
> *Gin makes a woman wanna fight,*
> *then fuck, then cry*
> *Crystal meth*
> *makes a boy think he can fly*
>
> *Gonna buy me an airplane*
> *fly all over your town*
> *Buy me an airplane*

fly all over your town
You know I'd fly right by your house
if I could just come down

Call him Sydney, babe
that's where I'll be
You can call him Sydney, babe
that's where I'll be
Oh lonesomeness
made a pleaser out of me

(Repeat first verse.
Outro: 12 bars, whistling.)

The last chord fades. He lets down the lid
on the friendly old Janssen and climbs off
the stage. With its fridge lamps and hanging
LEDs the bar is an island of light, a glassed
diorama. Perched atop a leatherette
stool, applying a match to a mint-green Sobranie,
his analyst grants him an almost imperceptible
nod. It's Bridget, still at work on the tills,
who manages an ironic round of applause.
'Señor Fandango' – cracking a Heineken,
sliding it to him along the bar, where Frank
mimes ¡salud!, takes a decorous swig –
'is the sentimental type, I think.' 'Why,
thank you. It's not everyone who gets it.'
And then, as if Bridget had posed him a
question: 'There's really just two kinds of
music lover. Some people understand
melancholy, some people don't.' Bridget,

absorbed in a pile of bank notes, counting
underneath her breath, slips the roll into
a ziplock bag. 'I can't disagree,' she
says, finally, 'but that's not what I meant.'

BOOK 2

CHAPTER 7

Even on dozy old Rock Oyster Island
laws of consequence apply. Arthur
and Marigold, idling away the morning
hours as best they can (bed-bound and
more than a little hungover, but sex,
he infers, being out of the question),
are summoned to account by a sonorous *bong*
from the wooden cowbell that hangs
on the porch: 'Anyone home?' pipes a voice
as the kitchen door creaks. Marigold
springs to and drags on a bathrobe. Arthur
and – equally crestfallen – Chuck avert their eyes
from her minatory glare. 'Harriet! What
a nice surprise' – meaning *what are you
doing in my kitchen, bitch?* – 'but how can I help?'
With a willowbark ointment, allegedly, to mollify
some fictitious allergy. 'Let's have a look
in the garage,' says Marigold in haste.
Reluctantly, like a bad-tempered Corriedale,
Harriet consents to be mustered. Or
a small mob, perhaps: for, yes, sheepishly
her two colleagues pick themselves out of

the shrubbery. 'Garden's looking good,'
remarks Christian, as Justin tucks away
his phone. Marigold lets up the roller
door of her makeshift dispensary and
locates the salve. Harriet, though, isn't
giving up yet. 'I'm sorry,' says she,
'but I'm busting. May I use your bathroom?'
It's worth a try, but she's missed her moment;
Marigold's back in control of her game.
'*I'm* sorry, Sweetie. The cistern's broken. You're
welcome to pee in the garden.' The young woman
scowls. 'Don't worry, these nice boys won't look.'
As one, the three turn their backs and vamoosh.

⚔

For Juanita, too, the aftermath of the Ball
brings a lingering sense of disquiet.
She reads, but she struggles to concentrate;
she walks to the store, but still brooding
on Frank. What was he up to, the suave
little prick, with that piteous matinée
idol routine? And why her reluctance,
with Bridget, to say how she feels about it?
God, how she misses those supervisions.
Luis would ease the anxiety from her, he'd
lift it, and then she could bear it herself.
A duty of care. Yes, but where *is* her duty,
if this Frank thing is going where she
thinks it's going: to her patient, okay –
but to her patient's others? To herself and
her lover? And if these fail to add up . . .

Damn it, Luis, why aren't you here?
But I am there, he'd say. I'm always there.
If you just didn't listen so hard, you might hear.

⚔

Too many prying eyes up at the Farm:
instead they convene at the Bali Hai
Tearooms, Joe nursing his second espresso,
Marigold chugging a reflective ale.
'All quiet at home, then?' 'I've locked them both in.
I'm telling you, those two are so fucking grounded!'
The anger, he knows, is mostly feigned,
but underneath lies real distress. 'So we need
him to write the thing, that's what you're saying?'
'You're the one who knows poets, Joe. But yes,
as far as I can see he's hell-bent on it
and bugger the rest of us. Isn't that
how the bastards roll?' 'Well, yes, pretty much.'
'So let's crack the whip, then. Make him
get the damn thing done. And maybe, if he can
just get it finished . . . what am I saying . . . ?'
He waits for the rest of it. 'Joe, do you think
he might put it aside?' 'Well, maybe, I guess . . .'
He casts about for some more plausible
consolation. 'Perhaps, on his own, when
he's no longer, you know' – 'Getting his
ashes hauled?' – 'Yeah, that – then maybe
he'll see what the rest of us see.' 'Talk to him
Joe. Do the bloke thing. He'll listen to you.'

⚔

71

'Well Chuck, me ol' mate, I guess this is it.
For the moment, I mean.' But the parrot
ignores him. Bardruin fastens the Gladstone bag
he's been stuffing with clothing. 'A few weeks
at most. I'll have this thing knocked off
before you can say "absurd mock-epic",
okay? That's a promise.' The bird rolls
its amber, irascible eye in the universal,
trans-species sign for *Whatever.*
'Come on Chuckles, you're just being childish.'
Nothing. He gives up, turns his attention
instead to the rubble of teacups and
ashtrays and screwed-up and scrawled-over
typescript that Marigold (not without irony)
describes as his 'work space' – bloody hell,
where does he even begin? – the sulking
bird just for the moment forgotten . . .

*Book him, Danno! Book him Danno! Escape
path lighting will guide you to your exit.*

'There you go, that wasn't so hard. I'll miss you,
buddy.'
          *Like I give a fuck. Hasta la
vista, Mister. A Big One! A Big One!!*

                              ⋇

Layers of antique cockleshells
give way softly underfoot; Bardruin
leans his weight on the transom, waits for a
small wave to lift them and shoves the craft

free. Clumsily he flops on board.
A few feet away in the nuggety dark
he can barely make out his lover's face.
Even so, Marigold keeps them in close
to the shoreline, tucked out of sight of the Farm.
Spiral galaxies of phosphorescence
flower with every sweep of the oars.

Finally, as they surf through the channel
between the tall rocks that stand guard on
the headland, Marigold puts an end
to the clammy silence. 'Chuck,'
she says drily, 'is going to miss you.
What about you, Mr Poet – are you
going to miss him?' Arthur, not to be
drawn either way, begins to whistle
'Sloop John B,' changes key for the Skye
Boat Song, then segues adroitly into
the Liebestod from *Tristan and Isolde*.
Stealthily now he picks up his bare, calloused
heel from the bait-stinky floor of the dinghy
and brings it to rest on the bench seat, amidships,
lodging it snugly in Marigold's groin.
'Hmm,' says the latter, noncommittal, as
her stroke brings her sliding into Bardruin's
hoof. Then 'Hmmm . . .' as her oars begin to dig
deeper, the bow slapping into the oncoming
chop – as she bends to her work – as her
stroke-rate increases – as the dinghy flies
forward like a horse that smells home.
'Row, row, row your boat,' her
insouciant passenger warbles *con brio*.

'Arthur Bardruin, you are . . . oooh . . . a complete
and utter . . . bastard, you know that . . . don't you?'

⚔

The cherry-red beacon of Joe's cigarette
guides them into a pebbly beach. While the others
climb out, he steadies the prow, then helps drag
the dinghy onto the shingle. Above them,
a flight of near vertical steps, blasted and gang-
bolted into the rock. One hundred and twenty,
Joe confirms, having counted them, switch-backing
steadily skywards, and these, with the poet's
meagre chattels divided between them, the trio
must climb: Joe in the lead, with a carton
of papers propped on a chilly bin packed
with victuals; Arthur, complaining, with
bedding and clothes; and lastly Marigold,
donkeying the Smith Corona. 'Did you ever
see that Herzog film, what was it called again?'
'This is not helping.' 'They drag this –' 'Yes, we've
seen it, Arthur, now for Christ's sake will you
shut the fuck up!'
                    Summiting, they arrive
at the door of a rumpty-looking fibrolite
shack. Anchored under the brow of the ridge, on
the scrubby side, screened from the rest of the property,
it doubles as man cave and spillover
fishing-gear-and-tool-shed. Joe puts a match to
a kerosene lamp which illuminates
in its jaundiced beam a potting bench,
a spartan cot, a graveyard of tackle and

appliances, and a weather-beaten card table.
'Behold, the lair of the ruined bard,' remarks
Arthur. 'I'm sure I'll feel right at home.'
'Don't get too comfortable,' Marigold
warns him. 'And whatever you do, keep your
head down. Okay?' 'On a good day,' puts in
the ex-instructor, 'you can see the Isle
of Drunks from here.' 'Did you hear that, Arthur?'
Marigold halts at the top of the staircase.
'*Think about it*. And think *about me*, you
bastard poet. Joe, I'm leaving you in charge.'

CHAPTER 8

'I seemed to be living at Manly Beach.
It's odd, I've never actually been there –
but that was the name that was in my head –
a huge old villa, Queenslander style, you
know, all those deep verandahs, red iron roof
and mango trees in fruit, and jacaranda
blossom. People were milling around with drinks,
I was hosting some kind of music fair –
like a garage sale, except all I was selling
was instruments. Melissa was there,
she was playing a piece, on piano, which
isn't her thing, of course. You've got good
at that, I told her; she said: I've been
dieting on it. There was so much junk,
there were whole rooms filled with percussion
and brass, and Melissa was telling me
Anton – he was our friend from Melbourne, we
met him at the Conservatory – Anton was looking
for a new crash cymbal. I said, we need to
have sex, but there were too many people.

'And then there's a part where I couldn't
remember – I mean, *in the dream*, it was
like I'd blacked out – and people were leaving,
we'd sold out apparently, I looked in
these rooms and now everything was
empty. Melissa had set up a stall
in the bedroom, she had all this fruit, in preserving
jars, the old-fashioned kind with the screw-on
collars, and women were lining up outside.
She told me to go and find the "accountant" –
she used that word, but I knew what she meant.
I had to organise more stock, more
instruments, so I got on the ferry.
It's hard to describe: it was daylight still
but the towers in the city were
all lit up, and the Opera House
with a lightshow playing on the tiles.
Somebody said that the buses weren't running,
I had to walk to Double Bay, and all
along Oxford Street there were closing-down
sales. Then I was going up in a lift
and when the door opened (the type with
the cage) my mother was sitting at
a keyboard that sounded like a spinet.
I could see she was giving a singing
lesson to a girl, a woman, her face
was hidden but somehow I knew that it
had to be Karen – but Karen as a
child, she was tiny, maybe three feet tall.
My father was there, in his magistrate's
wig, leafing through a pile of papers – it
looked like some kind of music notation –

Puccini, he told me, it seemed to be called
"Leporello". I started to say it was
dark outside, it was too late now to get
back to the Shore. I was worried about
having left Melissa. My father said,
come in the kitchen, I'll warm you some milk.'

Juanita lets the silence deepen. She isn't
rehearsing, exactly; she's just making space.

'Your father was leafing through a pile of music.
Does Frank leave through music, I wonder?
There's a lot of leaving here.'
                                    Her client
pauses only a moment as he picks out a thread.

'The day I quit the Conservatory, I was
walking home through Royal Park and suddenly
something was wrong with my lungs – I couldn't
get air, I was literally crying in pain.
They diagnosed something at the hospital –
God knows what, it didn't sink in, I guess
I could tell for myself it was probably
hysterical. Then when I got out of
A&E I had to make a phone call and
break the news. Ouch! My mother was so
disappointed, the passive aggression –
Christ, it was just withering. And it
got to me, you know, I did feel scared.
But I'd been writing songs, I'd lined up
the players, I had the sound all sorted
out in my head. This is the band that I've

told you about – the one that got me
across to the States. It happened so quickly
it was almost too easy – I'd hardly
been on stage before – but we did the first
album, the single got airplay, the label
sent us out to LA to make another one . . .'

'You left your partner behind in Melbourne?'

'Melissa hung in at the Con, that's right –
the arrangement between us was pretty vague . . .
I must have had ideas of "fun" on the road,
though actually that side of things was just bleak.
Anyway, we cut the new record, we toured
the West Coast, and the punters quite liked it.
Not the right moment – the early eighties,
it wasn't the time to play country – but it all went
okay. Except Steve crashed the tour van, smashed
up his forearm, the bass player fractured
his pelvis. And that was the end of it.
I stayed a while; I had this warehouse
in Silverlake, any other time it would have
been a cool place. But not just then, I was
too messed up. Pain meds, you know,
familiar story – one thing led to
another. And so Melissa came over . . .'

'One thing led to another?'
                              She tries not
to labour the irony, but Frank isn't slow.

'Fair enough. It's true, I encouraged her.

79

Not *too* directly, but it didn't take much.
She was jealous, I guess, and she had this idea
that she might make a fiddler – she tried for
a while – but it's like with a lot of classical
players, improvising was a different
language. And I was, well, the thing
about coke is, you think you're doing
so much better than you are. Really, though,
it was all pretty dismal. I had a few
gigs, I was "taking stock", you know,
but mostly I was just taking drugs. So
Melissa – thank God! – pulled the plug. Went
back to the Con, and she aced it, of course, top
in her year group. Instant career. By the time
I got home she was set to become a soloist.'

'Just add water . . .'
                    'Sorry?'
                                'You were jealous.'

'No. Not of *that* career. Honestly,
it's an awful life: all that time cooped up
in hotel rooms, the endless practice,
the colourless people. Wall-to-wall fags and
neurasthenics . . . shit. I didn't mean that.
Sorry.'
            'Didn't mean what?'
                                'The bit about "fags".'

'But Frank, we *don't know* what you mean. This is
analysis, isn't it? That's why we're here . . .'

Frank says nothing, the moment passes.
She might have cut proceedings there – 'short'
sessions, she'd use them more, but she doesn't
always have the nerve. And there's something else,
it's in that dream, something that makes her nudge him
forward.
            'Let's not leave the story there. That
would be *mean*. What else have you got for me?'

Frank blows out a gust of breath.

'Melissa, *she* thought I was mean. But she
left, and that worked out okay. For her, I mean.
And I stayed on and – I've told you about it –
I wrote those jingles. Scads of money. Heaps
of blow – I got myself completely fucked up.
In the end a friend came through – transiting,
on her way to Britain – she managed to
push me onto a plane and I got home,
back to Sydney, managed a rehab. It wasn't fun
but I made it, I came out clean. After that
I just laid low, did a few months of therapy –
remember Philip? – also the odd bit of
studio work. But I put up the shutters,
I didn't play gigs. I got on this physical
fitness jag – yoga, swimming, lifting
weights – I was living the whole "recovery"
life. And I loved it. Except for the twelve-
step thing: the God stuff, all that "sharing"
crap. No way, man. It creeped me out.
I'd go because of Karen, that was all.
Karen had been in rehab with me,

boilerplate junkie, the whole nine yards.
Sydney was drowning in heroin, the industry
was a slaughterhouse. And Karen (did I
tell you this?) was a singer. A really good
singer, when she let herself be; she had
that sombre, torchy thing, but a lighter
side to her voice as well – I used to think
half Karen Dalton and half Karen Carpenter.
Anyway, she was cleaning up, and we started
doing some work together. And then, well, one
thing led to another –'
                      'Again.'
                              'Okay, I take
your point. But I really loved her, I loved
the effect she could have on a room, and
being part of that. It was all very "blues" –
there was that kind of aura: she sang
like a junkie, even clean. At home she was
funny, or she could be. We had lots
of laughs. But she started falling off
her programme, drinking, smoking a bit
of pot – no, strike that – *I* was smoking pot,
and that was more or less okay, but then
Karen picked up and it all went to shit.
To be honest, I don't like to think about it.
Darlinghurst got really mean: sleazy,
dangerous, out of control. We saw someone stabbed
in an alley and just looked the other way.
Karen was hanging with a Serbian dude
she was getting her gear from, a real piece
of work. She came home one night with her hand
stitched up, this nasty slash across her palm,

82

and she wouldn't explain, just pushed me away.
Long story short: I took the hint. I bailed.'

Frank trails off . . .
                            Does he want to be rescued?
The analyst leaves him to rescue himself.

'What I should have done, I know, is to
try to get her back in the rooms. Really,
I did try. I took her to meetings, made
her come with me, made her speak.
She still had a sponsor – a flaky chick,
but she tried as well; it's just that Karen
wasn't having it. Finally someone
took me aside, this counsellor dude who
was also a junkie, and more or less
told me I was wasting my time. He fed
me the usual twelve-step Kool Aid –
carry the message not the addict, your
own recovery comes first, all that
self-care bullshit – and maybe he was right.
Or maybe it's just what I wanted to hear.
Either way, I listened. I came back home.'

'And how's that working for you now, your
sponsor's message? Are you milking it still?'

'I'm back in analysis. What do you think?'

'What do *I* think? I'm not the judge, Frank. You are.'

CHAPTER 9

Marigold likes to work in the garden
before the day gets punishingly hot.
This morning there's even a hint of dew
as she picks herself a pint of strawberries,
ties up snow peas, patiently untangles
rock melon vines from the guava hedge.
Gloving up, she shakes together a furtive
batch of copper spray – not her style, but
for passionfruit only (the shitty brown
grease-spot) she makes an exception.

All in all, we might conclude, a not
disagreeable morning in paradise.

Yet Marigold, as she makes her way
down the gully, now dappled in sun,
to the pig run, is out of sorts. The sight
of a kingfisher diving – a blur of vanilla
and teal – and yo-yoing back to its branch
with a grasshopper pegged in its bill,
she regards with a shrug. A cane toad
squatting on the grassy track she place-

kicks summarily into the blackberries.
Thirty years ago this month, just a few
weeks beyond her twenty-first birthday,
here, in the sunniest spot in the gully,
she forked her mother's ashes into
the soil. But just think if Persia could see
her now – *Marigold, darling, you blonde
tramp!* – her indomitable sidekick,
her sister-daughter, undone by, of all
childish things, an incontinent bard.

The hogs come brawling around her feet
with their huffles and snuffles and their snotty-
nosed kisses. This morning, however,
is not the right time to be pinning their
benefactor's knee against the gatepost.
'*Faaark!!* You fucking little toe rags, I've had
just about enough of you! Do you think
I won't turn you into saveloys? Just
you try me!' A fearful hush envelops
the gully: four pairs of blackcurrant eyes
are cast shamefully downwards. When
finally Marigold relents, and turns out her
bucket of mash and molasses, even
then comes a tremulous pause – a shifting of
trotters, a twitching of ears – before, one
by one, four quivering snouts are lowered
self-consciously, timidly, into the swill.

Bridget wakes up discomposed. It takes
her a moment to remember why:
a using dream – another one – she was
drinking Bombay Sapphire with Paulie
Laulala. Details hover at the edge
of the light . . . Paulie was playing a thumb
piano, Koro was there . . . but the details
don't matter; what stays is the shocked
sense of hurt (she forgot! it's not fair!).
Later, relief (it was 'only' a dream),
but the uneasy feeling stays with her
as she gets up to pee. In the cramped
galley kitchen she fixes coffee, carries
it back to her storm-tossed bunk. Something's
not right with that dream, she thinks. Why
dream of liquor? 'Alcohol is a drug', etc.,
she gets all that, she leaves it alone,
but drinking is not what she misses, it was
never her thing. She works in a bar, for
heaven's sake! She fills people up with it
night after night, it isn't an issue, and yet . . .
and yet still she can feel it. It's there in
her body, the limbic shock, the *plink plink
plink* of the thumb piano, a grief like
the floor of her stomach falling away.

⚔

Early starts are not Joe's thing. Can he
help that he's still a professor at heart?
Of course he can't! So the day begins with
a cup of tea and an hour's gentle reading;

86

then a light-ish breakfast, the morning papers,
an email or two, a remedial doze . . .
By the time he feels ready to venture
outside (in his dressing gown, nursing a second
coffee), the sunlight is blazing, cicadas
are drumming, and Wanda's Yoga for Menopause
ladies, knee-pants lubriciously soaked in
sweat, are down-dogging strenuously
on the kikuyu sward. Harriet, too, has opted
this morning for the pleasures of al fresco
pedagogy. A stand of ancient pōhutukawa
guarding the clifftop that faces north
offers a green and thoughtful shade from
beneath which to contemplate the gulf's blue
sublimities. 'Writing/Nature' is the
seminar's theme, and Harriet's students
are hard at work. In a cross-legged crescent,
their backs to the vista, they palpate the screens
of their tablets with studious vigour.

And what of the other, the fugitive –
is Bardruin furiously scribbling
too? Sidling out of Harriet's eye-line,
Joe doubles back through the citrus grove,
ducks down the ridge and then picks up the clay
track that winds through the tree ferns to
Bardruin's priesthole. 'Oh for God's sake,'
mutters Joe, hypocritically, 'is the bugger
even awake?' For on first appearance
nothing stirs: the curtains are pulled to, the door
firmly closed. But what he mistakes for
the drumming of bees is – hang on – the

pounding of typewriter keys! Not only
is Bardruin wide awake (he discovers,
on sliding back the door), but, wreathed
in a thick fog of weed and cigar smoke,
stripped to the waist and dripping sweat,
he's driving the poor old Smith Corona
like a coalminer wrestling a pneumatic
drill. 'Jesus, Arthur, are you all right . . . ?'
he finds himself shouting above the din –
the tight space amplifies the sound – 'Arthur,
stop for a moment. Please . . .' Bardruin
turns to the doorway but doesn't stop typing.
'O pestilence-stricken multitudes!'
he cries, as a sheet of A4 paper
drifts to the floor like an autumn leaf,
there to join disordered dozens of its
kind. Joe pulls the curtains and opens a
window. Already Bardruin's typing again;
ping! goes the bell on the carriage return
and now the poet's whistling too. The shed's
like a furnace, it stinks of sweat, and mania
and whisky fumes. 'For Christ's sake, light
that thing outside' – Bardruin reaches for
a fresh cigar – 'if you blow yourself up,
mate, your mistress will never forgive me.'

Draped in a hippie-ish cotton sarong
Marigold stands on the doorstep, towelling
her hair. Bridget climbs from her station
wagon; the older woman collects her in a

blowsy embrace. There's a minor excursus –
a wardrobe malfunction – as a rose-nippled
boob makes the briefest escape. 'Temptress,'
Bridget teases her, at which Marigold
blushes, but happily. 'Darling, I wish!'

There's no edge to this – it's a friendship that's
never been clouded by sex – but it's not been
pure sunshine. A dozen years older than
motherless Bridget, daughterless Marigold
has played that part; has played it warmly,
generously, and yet not (so her conscience
reminds her) unfailingly well. It all goes
back to the days of Gaucho Airways,
to the toothsome Carlos, his dastardly
trompe l'oeil briefcase, and to Marigold's
dispensary. Her stint as a coke merchant
passed without incident (largely) and reaped
her a fat pile of cash. For a meth-head
like Bridget, however, it was all
too much fun. Nowadays she plies a more
circumspect trade (weed, and the odd bit
of this and that). But the shadow of
Bridget's addiction still lingers: it's here
in the kitchen with them now as Marigold
pours steaming coffee and Chuck on
his ladderback chair talks excitable
filth. 'You like your Auntie Bridget, don't you?'
Marigold coaxes. 'It makes a change. Poor
wee Chuck's been moping lately. Haven't you,
Chuckles? He misses his mate.' Inquiringly
Bridget widens her eyes. 'Tell Auntie Bridget,

then. Who's your new friend?'

                              '*El poeta borracho*',
replies Chuck. '*Ella lo desterró*'.

And so, in the course of the next half hour,
the sorry, preposterous tale unfolds:
all the way from the poet's first landfall
(for Bridget is yet to hear any of this)
to the shambles at the HRT Ball
and Marigold losing her shit with the hogs.

'Help me,' her listener demands, at length,
'do I laugh or cry? Chuck, what do you think?'
But the parrot, it seems, has gone
back to his sulk. '*Poesía*', the bird
says, '*tampoco me gusta*'.

                              ⚼

Bridget needs to get to her shift. It's true.
It's also a mild evasion. Lately
there's been a few of these – between herself
and Juanita, for instance. 'Everything'
is not 'just fine' (as she placidly assures
her friend): the using dreams and messed-up sleep,
skipping meetings, eating crap – it doesn't take
a psychoanalyst . . . The history
between them is part of the problem: it makes
Bridget careful of Marigold's feelings. Also,
there isn't a story, as such. There are images
and intuitions, tag ends of conversations;
mostly, though, just bad ideas, furtive and

feral, that, as Bridget well knows, need to be
flushed out into the daylight and –

Oh crap, is that the time . . . ?

Mid-afternoon at the Sandgroper
things are still quiet. A handful of tourists
are tippling sedately, outdoors, under
a canvas sail. Bridget's 2i/c,
Miriama, is perched on her knees on
a barstool, resupplying the top shelf.
'Hey,' she says, as she clambers down,
'that guy from the other night was in.'
'Huh?' (At least she can maintain the form.)
'The piano player. He was asking for you.'

Bridget pokes her head in the kitchen, finds
Wiki Laulala prepping swordfish steaks.
'Look at these, Bee. They got it last night on
Paulie's boat. They're fresh as.' Obligingly, she
oohs and aahs. But truthfully it makes Bridget
glum: you shouldn't eat billfish, they're too
prepossessing, it's like eating dolphin, or
tiger, or God. Miri, meanwhile, is
still on about Frank. 'It's funny,' she says,
'he hung round for a bit, I was trying
to decide if he's cute or not. I mean, he's
old and everything. But it's something
else, those eyes . . . it's like they're almost too blue.'

CHAPTER 10

Mid-morning, Monday, the week's first session,
and Frank's having trouble getting started.
The problem, he says eventually,
is he just got back on the early boat, he spent
the weekend on the mainland, he's shattered.
He guesses he'll have to talk about it.
He'd happily not. Or so he keeps saying.
The analyst, noting the false note, lets it pass.

'So here's the thing – I had a date. On Friday,
after I'd been up the hill. Well, when I say
"date", I mean with an escort –'
                                    'A sex worker?'
'A hooker, whatever. Sophie, her name is.
Her working name. I've seen her before
a couple of times, I like her a lot. She's a little bit
older – late twenties –'
                           'More than half your age.'
'Fair enough, yes. But she's kind of smart and . . .
"hot", I guess. Not to put too fine a point on it.

'Anyway . . . last week something turned up;
all of a sudden I had some cash. My publisher
called me – he'd placed a song with an advertiser,
out of the blue – and here was the cheque
so I thought, what the hell, let's spend it.

'There's an old friend – well, he's kind of a friend –
he's got a beach house out on the Coast.
He's a corporate lawyer, owns all sorts
of real estate; this place, though, is something
else, and he's always saying I should use it.
So that was the plan. I'd go for the weekend,
treat myself – blow the whole lot – it was
dirty money.'
                          '*Treat* yourself?'

                                              'Right! So I
picked up a rental, met up with Sophie
and we drove out on Friday evening.
The trouble was, after I'd finished with
Mum I felt dreadful, worse than I have for
months; by the time we got out to the beach
I was totally flat. I'm thinking, like, Christ
I've got this girl here, now I have to
entertain her. All I wanted was to be in bed –
alone, I mean. I was useless to anyone.
Luckily, though . . . did I say the place is
swept up? Well, it really is. Floor-to-ceiling
views of the surf, infinity pool, expensive
art, wood-fired oven in the courtyard: the whole
nine yards. But classy, nothing too grotesque –
the grand piano isn't white! And Sophie
was totally rapt; she thought the whole thing

was fabulous. So, we lay in the spa pool,
drank some bubbles, talked – well, that's to say
I talked –'
        'About your mother?'
                'Well, yes, as it
happens? Not very sexy, I realise, but it
did cheer me up. And Sophie was happy.
We ate at a pizza joint, strolled down the waterfront,
looked at the surf. Later I left her watching
a movie and crashed out. Slept like the dead.

'But in the morning I was fine – no, better
than fine, I felt really great – it sounds kind of
dumb when I say it, but it all seemed so
peaceful. Sophie had come up to bed in
the night; I woke with my face pressed into her
neck, we were breathing together, like somehow
we'd got into rhythm. I wonder, do
you ever get that feeling – you're fully awake,
but you can't move your limbs? Like you're
under anaesthetic. I lay there, it must have been
an hour. I was smelling her skin, there was
sun in the room, and the smell of her hair
warming up in the heat. I was paralysed,
right? But so awake! And just so grateful
to have her there. I let her sleep, then I
made us a great big breakfast and brought it
back to bed. Later we got up, went out
for coffee, walked on the beach, had
a swim. So that was Saturday afternoon . . .'

Frank trails off, as if he meant to make room –
like someone scooching across in bed, Juanita
thinks, but refrains from saying. Whatever she's
waiting for here is still keeping its distance.

'Saturday night, we partied hard. I'd laid
in food so I cooked a nice meal. Sophie
was sitting at the island bench on a barstool
drinking whiskey sours, posting pics
to her friends, playing DJ with her phone.
We drank some outrageously expensive
wine – we were both pretty drunk – and then
she announced she had this coke she'd been
saving up, just in case –'
                              'Just in case what?'
'I guess – just in case she had a really
good time? Or a really bad one? No,
I'm kidding, this was a good time, no
doubt about it, we were both really
up for it. Like I said, she's sexy as hell.
Also, how can I put it, ah . . . broad-minded.
More than me, I'd have to say: she
spooked me just a little bit. She wanted
to do that breath-play thing with the plastic
bag over her face – but I couldn't, it
scared me.'
                'Why? Did you think you might like it
too much?'
                'No! It was creepy, it freaked
me out. We did do some other stuff, though;
it was pretty great sex! And the thing with
the breath-play game, of course, from my point of

view, was she trusted me.'

                'She treated you
as if you were special. You weren't just a client.
You were touched by that?'

                  'Absolutely,
yes, I was. Also, she told me her real
name, Carla. Not that I used it.'

                      'Oh? Why not?'
'I just don't like the name.'

                'But if you did . . . ?'
'Well, maybe, yeah. But Sophie's pretty.
Carla's dumb.'

           'And Sophie isn't?'

                'Sophie? Not
remotely, no. She's quick, she's . . . anyway,
next morning, Sunday – we woke up late, of
course – it was all a bit tricky –'

                  'For the girl,
or her trick?'

                'For me. I was feeling pretty
wrecked. In fact I'd almost had enough; it
crossed my mind we could pull the plug, we could
simply go home. But I felt obliged. I'd paid,
of course – I'd paid her heaps! – it wouldn't
have been any skin off her nose – but it
didn't feel right. It was all too hard, so
we went back to sleep for a while. Then
when I woke up, Sophie, bless her, had
gone out and got tomato juice and made
Bloody Marys. I felt much better, we
got back in tune again, as it were. She'd
had her eye on this seafood place on

the waterfront, so we went down for lunch.

'When we arrived the place was full.
We had to wait at the bar for a table.
And while we were sitting there, who should walk in
but this couple I know, and of course they're,
like, "Frank!" David and Sarah their names are,
South Africans, friends from the time I was
married to Paula, I hadn't seen either of them
for years. So I introduced them –'
                                    'To Sophie?
Or Carla?'
                        'To Sophie, of course. Now, I
like these people, they're fun; so a table for
four came free, and I figured: what harm can it
do, we may as well share it. I told them
Sophie was a former student. Honestly,
not that it mattered so much – they're both
pretty loose, they wouldn't have cared –
but that was the story I gave them, we were
working on some songs. And the thing is,
Sophie picked it up: we improvised, we
filled in the details. She was a singer,
we made her gay, we gave her a partner
(called Carla!) and so on. Who knows, maybe
the others saw through it. But everyone
drank quite a bit, we had a fine old time.
Then the two of us went home, had more sex –
excellent sex – and that was the day. By
the time we woke up it was time to get
moving. Sophie helped with the cleaning up.'

'Housework not being part of the fiction –
perhaps it was more than you bargained for.'

'Correct. You can see where this is going . . .
Okay, so there we were driving home –
driving back to town, that is – and Sophie was
saying the things you do, like she didn't want
to go back to "real life" and so on. And then
she said: "Maybe we could do this again?"
And I was, like, "Sure!" or "That'd be great",
or something, and she said: "You wouldn't
have to pay." We'd had a joint, which didn't
help – my reactions were a bit out of sync,
the way they can be – and I said: "Oh no,
I'd need to pay." Or I might have said, even,
"I'd *much rather* pay." Whatever I said,
it wasn't right. I knew it the moment I said it,
but . . . Sophie didn't say a thing; she didn't
bite back, just closed up. Played with her phone.'

The analyst waits, but he says nothing more.
She knew where the story was going – Frank
was right – and now it's gone there.

'What was the thing you should have said? If your
timing was better.'
                    'What could I have said?'
'It depends what you felt.'
                    'I felt touched, as you put it.'
'Yes, but what *else* did you feel?'
                    'I felt anxious.'
'Yes . . . ?'

98

'And shamed. The last thing I wanted
was to hurt the girl's feelings.'
                                    'Even so,
you tricked her into breaking your treaty.
You *got* what you wanted' –
                              'That's a bit tough!'
– 'except for the fact that you didn't want it.'

                    ⚔

The analyst sits at her writing desk with a case
file open in front of her. HORTUNE, Frank.
She unscrews the cap of her fountain pen, writes:
The analyst's ear is a recording device.
She opens the french doors, lights a cheroot.
The analyst's cards are face-up on the table.
Harriet Whitbread jog-trots past on
the duckwalk, bouncing a volleyball.

The analyst isn't a moral instructor,
a life coach, a priest, or an agony aunt.
No one can come to the phone right now.
Please leave your message after the tone.
It isn't a question of liking the patient;
the task is to love them. As simple as that.
In a blizzard of signs, in an ambush of furs,
she pays out her line through a hole in the ice.

CHAPTER 11

His handlers, putting their heads together,
determine that Bardruin needs a day off.
A picnic, for instance. Joe's part in this:
to deliver the poet to the church on time.
(Joe to Marigold: 'Only that, you say.
What's the singular of herding cats?')
And yet when on the appointed morning
he rattles the door of the garden shed
he finds the incumbent not merely awake
but apparently sober, with hot water
bubbling on the gas ring. Turning valet,
the ex-professor furnishes (from a
sporty daypack) soap and razor, toothbrush,
flannel, underwear and a crisp clean towel;
cunning deployment of pots and buckets
soon has Bardruin pinkly scrubbed. Next,
to a preppy-looking foldaway suit bag,
unzipping which Joe extracts, by degrees, an
improvised statement in writerly beachwear –
makeshift, it has to be said, yet demonstrably
chic: *viz.*, tennis creams, of significant
vintage, hitched in place with a silk tie;

a faded, once-pink cotton shirt, sun-bleached
and softened like the fuzz on a peach,
and teamed with (*Whoah, check this out!* –
where does Marigold find these things?)
a blazer styled in artfully crumpled
moss-green linen, by Tommy Hilfiger.
Footwear takes the voguish form of the poet's
preferred *sandales romaines*. And, crowningly,
from Joe's own wardrobe – souvenir of his
teaching days, frayed, distressed and sweat-
besotted – a panama, with a walnut band.
'How do I look?' asks the made-over subject,
refining the set of his hat brim minutely.
'You look,' replies Joe, 'like a million bucks. Like
Somerset Maugham! Like the Poet on Holiday!!'

It remains to escort him to the foot
of the staircase where Marigold's dinghy
is parked on the gravel. 'Taxi for Bardruin,
Arthur,' says she. Her passenger rolls up
his elegant strides, pockets his sandals
and clambers aboard. 'Give us a shove, will
you, Joe. I'll have him back before curfew.'

⤜

The morning is windless, the sea like oil;
outcrops of cumulus boil on the distant
horizon. Here and there small knots of wheeling
seabirds mark the locations of feeding fish.
A gannet plummets from vertiginous

altitude, crashes into the water beside them,
bobs to the surface, tipping its throat back,
shaking its sulphur-bonneted head.

Their destination is a rocky protrusion
that rises abruptly a mile offshore. From his
seat on the stern bench, Bardruin peers as
it slowly takes shape over Marigold's shoulder –
from this angle, ugly, intimidating
even: haunches of grimy basalt
and salt-crusted pine trees. 'Trust me,
just wait' – Marigold, tracking the line of
his gaze, his uncertain expression;
the thirsty poet makes an easy read:
'Try that ice bin, sweetheart, under your feet.'

With half an hour's effort they're in reach of
the outcrop. Marigold puts up her oars
and leaves the dinghy to drift. As Bardruin
burrows again in the party ice, hooking out
happily a brace of ales, the other
takes up a spinning rod and tosses a
garish-looking softbait over the stern.
Seigneurial, the poet lounges, savouring
piney American hops. Then: 'Ho! What's this?'
For now he discovers, patting the pockets
of his elegant blazer, a stowaway: *to
wit*, a prodigious Montecristo. 'Oh, my God!'
Gales of smoke soon envelop the small craft –
bitter chocolate, liquorice, clove. 'Happy,
are we?' Marigold asks, superfluously;
then her rod tip bends double. 'Hold

this beer, will you. Here comes lunch . . .'
She wrestles the fish off the rocky bottom,
horses it up to the surface and scoops
it on board. Flamingo-pink, darkening
to bronze at the shoulders, the big snapper
flaps in the dinghy's bilge. As Bardruin
raises his beer in salute, she skewers
their catch through the brain with a steel spike.

⚔

Some days everything just goes right: the sun
pours down, the ocean drips from the blades
of the oars like Venetian glass; a shag
zips by on its private freeway, fifteen
inches above the water. And here, on
the seaward side of the islet, the cove,
which is empty, and still, and unchanged.
As the dinghy rides on a bulge of swell
through a narrow chute between house-sized rocks
and skates out into a jade lagoon
no larger than half a football field,
the poet can only clamp his jaws round
the tuck of his Montecristo and applaud.

⚔

A driftwood fire, in a cage of stones,
has bedded down into pristine coals. On
a wire mesh grill are strewn red bell peppers,
corn (in the husk) and radicchio. The snapper –
filleted, scaled and scored, black-peppered,

lightly filmed in oil – waits its turn on a
plate in the ice bin; so too a ripe rock
melon, and a Margaret River sémillon.

'My mother used to bring me here,' says
Marigold. 'This was our secret place.
I don't often share it, you understand.'
'I do,' says Bardruin, cautiously. With
their backs to a boulder, cradling beers, they
recline hip to hip in the powdery sand.
'School days, week days, those were best;
she'd write me a note and we'd skive off
together. This is where I learned to row.
She'd be snoozing, reading books, and I'd scull
up and down, up and down . . .' 'Busting out
of school for the day? It sounds a bit like
you and me! But darling, *please* don't make me
paddle that great heavy boat, I'm far too old.'
Marigold laughs at him. 'Get you rowing?
That's the last thing that's going to happen.
You think I want you escaping on me?
I warn you, Señor Poet, that is not the plan.'

⚔

Gentle reader, sooner or later, you know –
and I know – it has to be told. So what
better time and place than this: on a spongy
bed of kikuyu grass, with the perfume
of kānuka thick in the air, with kererū
cooing and billing in the fuchsias,
Marigold spreading the picnic blanket and

Bardruin whistling rakishly '*Cinque* . . .
dieci'?

      In his studied opinion,
Marigold's cunt tastes of honeysuckle, gun
flint and crème brûlée; tropical fruit notes;
mouthfeel, silky with (yes) just a hint of Bluff
oyster astringency. Mind you, he's not exactly
spitting and rinsing – guzzling, rather, like
the drunkard he is. And does Marigold
like to be guzzled? You bet! She also
enjoys, immoderately, the sway-backed
curve of Bardruin's dingus, the way that
its firm but thoughtful stroke (with a subtle
camber of hips to match) gets to precisely where
she lives, yes there, and there, and there, and fuck me
there.

      We could go on (the lovers do – they're old,
they know how to make this work!). Yet the measures
on which they are now embarked – their fitness
and fullness, their metrical pulsion – will carry
them safely from here to there without our
anxious supervision. We can leave them,
reader. You have my word: form is
observed without haste or omission, till
the kererū, pooping in fright, take wing
and the stanza arrives at its paroxysm.

⟨⟩

When at length the lovers rouse and
unstick themselves, the tide is still full.
Schools of tiny translucent baitfish

fracture on the glittering sand;
a stingray slides into deeper water,
shuffling a layer of silt from its wings.
Some days everything just goes right.
As if Nature had drawn them a lagoon-sized
bath, they lounge chest-deep in its drowsy
warmth (Marigold, to complete the impression,
sluicing Bardruin's gloop from her crotch).

'What's that noise? Can you hear that?'
                                    Faintly,
yes, there's a distant whine, like a blowfly
buzzing at the edge of sleep, like a neighbour's
skillsaw, a mid-morning leaf-blower, something
small and silly like that . . . but louder, getting
closer, dammit, there's no doubt about it,
it's coming this way, until – *Oh no,*
you have got to be kidding me! – blasting
out of the rocky slit, in a blaze of
Miami pink and powder, trailing a rooster tail
of froth, it's *wouldn't you know it* a fucking
jet ski! Open-mouthed, the bathers gape as
it hammers across the lagoon towards
them, slams side-on at the final moment and
slides to a bobbing halt at ten yards' distance.

Simon Richwhite cuts the engine: 'Ahoy
there, nature lovers,' he cries. 'Is this
the most wicked place, or what? And can
you believe it, there's no one here!'
As if he'd dashed it off himself in an idle
moment at his drafting table, the architect

spreads his sculpted arms, gathering all he
surveys in his modest embrace. 'Enjoy!'
he tells them, indulgently. 'Don't do anything
I wouldn't do.' Then he fires up the hideous
beachtoy and fishtails away again.

'Where were we?' Marigold almost says,
but doesn't: it isn't as simple as that.
The engine noise thins out and dies, the spent
fuel clears, the bow-waves settle; but the day
as it now reassembles itself is not
the warm bath they were languishing in.
Perfection – ask any child on its birthday,
ask any parent (ask any poet!) – hangs
by a hair above fathoms of grief. Right
now, somebody needs to be Mother.
'Arthur' – demurely she crooks her finger –
'come here, lover, I've something for you.'
And so she does: for the kindly waters,
stirred up, lapping around her waist, have
wafted to hand the magic salve, the gold
kintsugi resin to patch up their day.
Stealthily, in her cradled palm, she nets
the gobbet of bardic jism. 'Hey, you fucking . . .
don't you dare! You witch!' the author squeals –
in vain – as Marigold smears the healing
unguent lavishly through his Grecian curls.

CHAPTER 12

Juanita and Bridget have been here before,
it's built in at ground level: call it
the Shady Grove factor. To come from
such utterly different worlds (to hell with
the neighbours, the bourgeois decorum)
is all quite delightful – except
when it isn't. And party nights out in
the Swamp are a case in point.

Every six months or so, therefore, they . . .
what? 'Quarrel' isn't the right word exactly.
But the discord's a worry and its roots descend
deep into places where neither of them
wants to start digging. Briefly, Juanita
will not go to Shady Grove. The scene
in the Swamp makes her shy and self-conscious
('common touch' not being one of her gifts).
Bridget, she rightly assumes, feels judged, but
the best that Juanita can do is plead weakness:
'Darling, you know what it's like for me.
The Argentinos won't show up, Jonah and Sigrid
aren't going. Who do I talk to? You'll have

your friends, with their drugs and the rest of it.
I'll just be tied to your skirts, feeling wooden.'

All of which is entirely true, and none
of which Bridget is ready to listen to.

'Please, Juanita, just this once. I know
you don't want to but . . .'
                              Just this once?
Juanita catches herself, but barely. 'It's just
me, *cariño*. Honestly, you'll have more fun
without me.'
                    'I won't!'
                              'You will! I'll wait up
for you.' And so on, mechanically, rising
and falling, like carousel ponies: the Belle
of the Boglands, Ms Bridget O'Dwyer, and
the esoteric Ice Queen of Plaza Güemes.

                              ⚑

The bayou *thang*. It's mostly a joke, but
no one has ever told Leo the Crab Man.
He putters about in his Florida fanboat;
he lards his speech with creolisms; and
by the time Bridget has made her way home
from her unsatisfactory debate
with Juanita, he is well into fixing
the lavish confection which long ago
earned him his nom de guerre, that staple of
southside party fare that is Leo's notorious
paddlecrab gumbo. A sawn-off 44-gallon

drum does duty as a fat-arse kettle.
'Smells good, Leo,' Bridget says. And truly,
just for the moment, it does: pork sausage,
celery, green pepper, fennel, commingling
their juices enticingly. It's only those damned
crabs, bitter and fleshless, which Leo
invariably adds by the bucketful – 'Look at
the meat on those critters, cher!' – that scare
away all but the most drunk, or kindly.

This evening, however, relief is at hand:
Leo's new friend is on board to restrain him.
Spawned in a tract home in Natchitoches,
schooled in the dive bars of Baton Rouge,
Willow Durst may be a hippie flake but she
knows her Rockin' Dopsie from her Boozoo
Chavis. She's also coming to grips with Leo:
'Come on pumpkin, we've got all those fish heads
and scallops and clams, you can hold the crawdads.
Just for me? Hey, tell you what' – hoisting
the bucket of grumpy crustacea – 'let's
go and drink some of Bung-Eye's hooch!'
Which is what they do. And as the twilight
thickens, and the tide starts to fill beneath
Bung-Eye's deck, Willow stealthily decants
the vital ingredient into the swamp.

Beneath the shoreline macrocarpas – wired
with spots and fairy lights – improvised trestle
tables sag beneath mountains of assorted

kai. Down the track comes Captain Blood with a
wheelbarrow, toting a massive kingfish.
Barbecue-meister Wiki Laulala tends
to a hogget on a charcoal spit. When
Marigold arrives, on dusk, she unloads a
brace of smoked kahawai and a carton
of melons. From the vantage point of his
mistress's shoulder her feathered familiar
peers left and right. 'Has my friend been
forgiven, then?' Bridget inquires. But Chuck
is in no mood for pleasantries. '*¿Dónde está
el maldito mestizo?*' the parrot demands,
and by way of reply, along the gangway from
Bung-Eye's cabin, bouncing on his three good
legs, comes the mongrel in question, his ancestral
foe. 'Boof!' remarks Homebake, provocatively –
and bolts, with the bad-tempered bird in pursuit.

'Come on darling, let's get you a drink,' suggests
Bridget. They settle themselves on her deck,
observing the revellers gradually filling
the party zone, while the sunset deepens,
first salmon, then scarlet, then cooling
to ash as a velvety darkness seeps
out of the mangroves. 'So, then – no Juanita
tonight,' says Marigold, finally. 'Is that okay?'
'I guess so. I don't know,' says Bridget.
'Why can't I simply roll the dice? Women,
men, the Swamp, the city – Jesus, girl, just
pick a side! Is it greed, I wonder? I tell you
what, though – I'm damned if I'm going to feel
alone at my own party.'

'You're not alone,
babe. I'm flying solo, too, remember?
I'll be your date.'
          They mark the deal with
a smooch, a hug, a toast, and then bestir
themselves. For the driving rattle of Groober's
banjo has just been joined by a squalling fiddle.
'That,' says Bridget, 'must be Constable Dave.
'Come on, my gorgeous date. Let's do it.'

⚹

On the grassy bank down by Cooch and
Groober's, spilling up over their duckwalk
and deck and onto Leo's pontoon (rafted
up alongside), the party is finding its sea legs
in double quick fashion. Raucous hillbilly
dance music helps and the Shady Grove Allstars
are giving it heaps. Most of whom, by this
stage, need no introduction:
          Ladies and Gentlemen –
all the way from the Swordfish Club, on tea
chest bass, that's *Paulie Laulala!* On washboard,
Koro Bill. Strumming guitar tonight, *Mr
Frank Hortune*. In the bottle-green shades,
on piano accordion, everyone knows
Manfred Singleton; likewise our hard-working
string-players, *Groober* and *Dave*. Then there's
the big guy expertly steering his golf
buggy into the firelit circle, nobody's fool
on the blues harmonica – from the Pearly
Shells Rest Home, it's *Wayne the Larger!*

And last but not least, with his mandolin
dwarfed in his meaty paws as he chops out
the backbeat, please give it up now for
Slippery Bob (an ordinary picker
but the finest meth cook on the island).

A roster of venerable hoedown standards
soon has the place in a thirsty sweat.
'Arkansas Traveler', 'Nine Pound Hammer',
'Big Sandy River', 'Cotton-Eyed Joe':
anyone who says you can't boogie to
bluegrass doesn't know the good folks of
Shady Grove – or the strength of Bung-Eye's
feral tequila, travelling hand to hand
in a three-litre juice bottle. Crawling
out of their caravans, their yurts, their coal
bins, their shipping containers, from their
cardboard huts in the bamboo thickets, from
their shanties of plywood and rusty iron,
they've come – the Southside rank and file,
every last woman, man and mutt – to join
and testify together at this ramshackle
outdoor cathedral of Good Clean Fun.
There *must* be a God. Just listen to that
stomp! Just check out those beards and
bandanas and bush shirts, the fishnets
and ponchos, the white Affco gumboots,
heaving together in their boggy *esprit
de corps*. Through a haze of weed and tobacco
smoke, of biker sweat and spitroast fumes,
the lonesome sounds of Appalachia
weave their counterfactual joy.

When Groober calls a five-minute breather
his Allstars dematerialise. For the sensible
(e.g. Koro Bill, taken in hand by his sensible
spouse) there's time to pile up a plate of kai
and tame the effects of Bung-Eye's 'shine.
Manfred and Groober share a sensible joint.
But Slippery Bob lights out for his vehicle –
hotly pursued by a vigilant Cooch,
by Wayne in his golf cart, by Constable
Dave, by Paulie and (*Fuck it all, why not?*)
Frank. 'Buckle in. Next stop Breakdown City,'
says Manfred, drily. Groober nods. 'You mean
Dave and his bloody landspeed-record
fiddle tunes? There should be a Law . . .'

For now, however, as Bridget and Marigold
join the pickers around the bonfire,
everything's calm. On Marigold's shoulder
Chuck appears to have fallen asleep. Likewise
his adversary, draped on a haybale, head
laid serenely in Bung-Eye's lap. Yet one ear
still twitches. And Groober need no more than
plink-plonk his way through a certain key phrase
to find the mutt quivering beside his knee
in the pitch perfect likeness of a dog
being good. 'Shall we do the song, then?'

(With a tasteful squeeze of accordion
and spectral plucking . . .)

Oh Shenandoah, I long to see you
Ow-wowww *you rolling river!*
Oh Shenandoah, wow-wow-owww-woo-woo
Wow-woww, *I must* oo-woooo
Across the wide wow-woo-woooo*!*

Tears stream from underneath Manfred's glasses;
Bung-Eye struggles vainly to conceal his pride.
Even the somnolent bird can't deny it:
'¡El mestizo canta con gran duende!'

Here and there the implacable physics
of dissipation exacts its toll. Not so much
among the drug-deranged pickers: well
after midnight the tempos bear witness
to the virulence of Slippery Bob's
wares. The fan base, however, begins
to erode. Mud-wrestling, bullshitting,
losing the car keys, sedentary drinking
account for their share; broken boot-heels,
twisted ankles . . . Even Bluey Winters
runs out of puff. A wiry old coot with a
flaming mohawk, Bluey (knocking on
85) is famed for his kindness,
his priapism, and the brio
of his antic bush carpentry. He is credited
too – collaboratively, with his
winsome enabler Vanessa Thrush –
as author of some of the freakiest dance
moves ever attempted this side of the island.

115

But could it be Bluey is feeling his age?
With Bridget and Marigold, Leo and Willow,
observing like dowagers from Bridget's
deck, the couple nurse drinks and make low-
voltage chatter. Even so, Bluey soon
warms to a signature theme.
                                        'Read your Lawrence,
boys and girls – and stop watching porn,
you'll over-think it. *In through the cunning
and out through the titties!* The Dao of
Rooting? It's all about Chi.' His lover
extends a prehensile arm and winches
him in by his scrawny neck. 'Nice in theory,
Rooster Boy' – laughing, teasing his
scarlet comb – 'but there's not been much
peace in the barnyard lately.' 'That's a bit harsh,'
Bluey says. But he beams like the Buddha.

⚔

Now down the jetty comes June Te Patu.
Bridget, easing her chair back, stands up to
greet her. 'Lovely party, Bridget dear. But
this old lady needs her beauty sleep. Koro's
still going. I wonder' – this to Marigold –
'darling, would you mind?' Three handsome
women (and one dozy parrot) make their way
up to the dusty road. Bridget hands June
into Marigold's truck, then circles round
to the driver's window. 'Promise me you'll come
straight back.' 'Of course I will. I'll take Chuck home,
but an hour at most, okay? I'm still your date!'

116

Bridget watches the plume of dust as it
bubbles along the chalky road, drifting,
almost imperceptibly, spilling
out over the mangrove flats. The full
moon, sailing clear of the pine trees,
glares down bright enough to read by.
Kānuka gives off its summery heat smell,
perfumed, off-dry: ginger and honey.
Up here – even with all the bikes and vehicles
bunched along the verge – the party sounds,
the hints of light, arrive as if from miles away.
Crickets louder than the music. Louder
than someone shouting, drunk and happy.

An hour at most, Marigold promised, and meant it.
The problem, however, is Auntie June:
inevitably she has picked up a
whisper, and now she requires to hear it
from the horse's mouth. Accompanied, as
might be imagined, with hoots and cackles
and good-natured chidings, the drowned-poet
story must be told in June's kitchen
with pikelets and serial cups of tea.

When at last she gets back to the Swamp
she finds the party in its twilight.
A dozen-odd bodies are slumped round
the fire, there's laughter from Bung-Eye's
kitchen. And yes, there's still music.
But even here the ranks have thinned:

no sign of Dave or Slippery Bob; Big
Wayne nodding off at the wheel. No
Frank either: it's Manfred and Groober
with Koro noodling on Frank's guitar,
a whacked-out, spacey and structureless jam
to gladden the heart of the dopiest
Deadhead . . . which might well be Marigold –
just her thing – were it not for the pulse of anxiety
drumming in her abdomen. And written, it
must be, all over her face, so that looking
up Manfred reads it at once; with the tilt of
an eyebrow he points her to Bridget's boat.

In the shadow of Leo's water tank Marigold
freezes. The cloudy flask, and this –
initially, hopelessly – is her only thought,
could almost be the moon reflected mistily
in the rising tide. But the real moon's light
is too concise for the comfort of ambiguity:
there is no mistaking the Zippo flame,
no disguising Frank and Bridget,
no unseeing the river of smoke that
drains from his mouth into hers. The pale
arc of Bridget's throat; his face in shade;
the glass bowl fuming. And Marigold
trapped in the shadows, aghast and ashamed.
She can no more step forward, declaring
herself, than if she were watching them
making love. As she buries her face in
her hands she can still taste the sweetness.

BOOK 3

CHAPTER 13

In a tucked-away corner of the Bali Hai
Tearooms, Joe Bravo plays with his ballpoint
and stares out the window. The routine
survives from his teaching days. Forced
to confront some dreary assignment no
longer able to be postponed – a thesis
report or a reference to fake for a dimly
remembered former student – he'll bribe himself
with a leisurely stroll through the village
and a ceremonial brunch. This morning
a bonus: the lovely Conchita, pulling
a shift for the opposition, sauntering
by with the water jug, a menu and her
incomparable smile. *'Buenos días,
profesor,'* she tells him. He basks
for a moment in the unearned attention.

Right now, however, he could take or leave
this twilight of the once-and-former. (Just
when you thought you were out, they
drag you back in!) How many times has that
unthinking pleasantry – 'Sure, send it through

and I'll have a quick look' – come back to sink its
reproachful fangs in his lazy, pusillanimous
arse? The typescript that squats at his elbow
is fully an inch thick. Not that he isn't
curious. And the author – let's not forget –
is his friend. But how can it possibly not
end in tears? And what is he, Joe, supposed
to do about it?
                         With the opening door
comes a sprinkle of noise from the street outside –
he looks furtively up – but it's only young
Frank, the musician, who politely ignores him.
Right then. He picks up the fat pile of
manuscript, tamps it square on the tabletop.
He sips his coffee, licks his finger, turns
down the blank cover sheet and reads:

          ESCAPE PATH LIGHTING
              a South Seas fantasia

          by Arthur Bardruin

                      ✄

Frank has his own morning coffee routine.
It brings him here straight from his therapy
session. Armed with a short black, he'll plug
in his laptop and rattle down everything
Juanita just said. So spare, so hieratically
unforthcoming is the analyst in her
interventions that every scrap that falls

from her lips demands to be hoarded
just in case. Even today, with the week's
sessions cancelled (Juanita offshore on a
conference trip) he keeps up his vigil. His
dreams are so furtive, they need to be
nailed down in prose or they scuttle
like cockroaches into the darkness and –

'Frankie Boy!'
                    Oh, Christ. Wouldn't you know it?
Everyone else here leaves him in peace, but
pushy and tone-deaf, hide-like-an-elephant,
Simon Richwhite – *sigh* . . . Frank shuts
the computer. It's not just the architect's
uncanny knack of appearing wherever
he's wanted least, but his instinct for finding
precisely the subject that whomever he's
buttonholing least wants to talk about.
Thus, clearing space for his huevos
rancheros: 'Tell me, are you still on the couch
with the good Dr Díaz?' Frank, on his guard,
mutters something evasive. 'I know – it's
a foolish question, right? You're in for the long
haul, of course you are. We both know how
difficult it is to get free.' Appearing bemused
is a fatal mistake. Now Richwhite is going to
explain, and there's nothing Frank can do about it.
'I've been there myself, you see. Not with
your Sapphist, with someone in town, but
I got out, I'm telling you. Jeepers! I saw through
the play straight away, though. You know
why? The shrinks run the same con that we do!'

The architect pauses, partly to chew, and
partly to savour the moment, the theatre
of sharing it. 'Here's how it works. A client
comes in – a couple, let's say – they've got
eight hundred K. They say, "Here's what we want,
can you build that for us?" Well, you couldn't,
for twice that, but "Yeah, no problem." You tell
them it's tight, but because they've got taste –
they've got such a great project! – there's things
you can do: you'll call in some favours, shave
your own fees. And all this, of course, *just for
them*. Do you follow? What you're selling
these poor trusting souls is . . . themselves!
Because that's what they're shopping for, right?
Just like you. You go in one end as a
fucked-up depressive and you come out the other
as a French Intellectual!'
                            'I don't know that –'
'Come on! I'm pulling your tit. But stay with
me here, we're just getting to the good part.
Here's where you groom them: you wine them and
dine them, you pore over magazines with them
like colleagues, you walk them through places
they could never afford in a dozen sorry
lifetimes . . . you get the idea. Then you
hit them with "drawings", as we call them
euphemistically: full computer modelling, a 3D
environment. Squire them through it, room by
room – it's all there, every last must-have
accessory. Check out that too-chic industrial
track lighting. Love that adobe pizza oven.
Ooh, is that a Judy Millar? Nice! And hang on –

who's this here, this couple in the Japanese cedar
tub? Is that . . . ? "Who's that? *That's you.*" "That's us!"
Ka-ching. It's a beautiful thing, my friend.'

'Simon, you really are something else,' says
Frank, without emphasis. Richwhite laughs.

'A day or two later they get the first invoice
and fuck me dead they've spent eighty-five K!
So what do they do? Do they scream blue
murder – remember, you've not done a jot
of real work! – do they chalk it all up as
a valuable life lesson, bail out,
write off the money they've spent? I tell you,
I've never seen it happen. It's too late:
they're hooked, you just reel them in. *Now* you start
work on the plans themselves – months of it, Frankie
Boy, beautiful gravy. They realise it's going
to cost twice what they thought – so what?
The only way out is to build. It's too
big to fail! It's humiliating, too.
And if they come on all niggardly – start to
push back – then "Look," you tell them (I love
this bit) – "look, I can build you a pile of
crap, we can save you some cash. But if
you want something stylish . . ." Fools and their
money, Frank. Squeeze, and keep squeezing.
On a good job, you milk half the budget in fees.'

Frank's at a loss as to what tone to strike.
It's a joke, right? He's meant to be a good
sport about it. Really, he'd like to take a shower.

125

'Nice story, Simon, but you're going to
have to help me. What's it got to do with –'

'Your therapy? Frank, don't play dumb. Work
with me: let's say you've been with Juanita for,
I don't know, what is it now, six months? So . . .
what would it cost – and I mean, *really* cost –
if you pulled the plug now? Well, there's six
months of fees (say, a thousand a week?), but hey,
that's just the money. It's the other bit
that guts you: the pride, the attachment, the entire
goddamn *project* of it. What if it's really
a crock of shit? Ah, but of course, there's
the progress you've made. Already!
That's right, and it's a long campaign, you've been
laying the groundwork, and sooner or later . . .
But *how* soon, I wonder? In one year? In
two? There's a name for it all this, it's
called the sunk cost fallacy. Look it up,
buddy, you can read all about yourself.
Don't get me wrong, though, it isn't
the money: it's *you*, it's the work, it's that
self you've invested in. Oh, and the lightbulb
that's just round the corner. Already paid for!
The Jewish Science, Frank, ain't that something?'

Richwhite pushes back his chair. 'I'll let you
you get back to your homework, shall I?'
Confidingly he squeezes Frank's forearm:
'Don't leave before the miracle happens!'

✖

126

With an untapped bottle of single malt
and the fateful manuscript tucked up his jumper –
fortified by a pep talk from Sigrid
('for heaven's sake, husband, just slap some sense
into him') – Joe climbs down through the kānuka
to beard the author in his lair. He discovers
him draped, unclothed, on a deckchair
sunning himself an indelible bronze.

'Arthur Bardruin, take a bow! You've excelled
yourself, maestro. I laughed like a drain.'

A rummage producing a brace of teacups,
Joe pours monumental drinks. 'To
you, my friend, and your mighty fantasia!'
He drags out a fish bin by way of a seat.
'Goodness me, it's terrific work. Definitive,
even . . .' *Get on with it Joe.* 'But Arthur –
I realise this goes without saying, but even so –
promise me you won't try to publish it.'

Joe has that sense of observing himself,
from a great distance, caught up in something
unspeakable. Not one for masking his feelings,
the poet looks stricken. 'You don't understand,
Joe, I *had to* write it.' He semaphores
helplessness, slopping his drink. 'It's out of my hands –
it's like the poem wrote itself. I woke up
one morning and the whole thing was *there.*'

Joe understands this. He really does. But
it's also the problem, does Arthur not

see? The spirit moves and the hapless poet
gets blown away. They despise that stuff.
'Diminished responsibility, Arthur –
seriously? It's a crime in itself! You're meant
to be showing the Muse who's boss, for God's
sake. We're dealing with schoolmasters here.'
'But you liked it, Joe!'

                              'I did. I do! But I'm
just an old man tending his cactuses, gone
in the right brain. Gone in the taste buds.
Truly – if it were up to me – your transports,
your side-spin, your middle-aged priapism . . .
mate, you're speaking my language here! But
nobody else is, you see, that's the problem: it's
called history, Arthur; you can't argue with it.'

To this point the victim has been doing
his best: an appearance of listening,
of taking it gamely. But this crap
about 'history' is one hurt too many.
Bardruin chokes on his Glenlivet, loses
it completely. *'History?* Holy
Mother of Christ! Those little shits wouldn't
know history if it sat up and barked at them.
What the hell were you teaching those kids –
how to write their motherfucking grant
applications? What about memory, eh professor?
What about Keeping the Romance Alive?
What about Malcolm Lowry gargling
shaving lotion? You and your cactuses!
You want to know your problem, Jonah Bravo?
I'm telling you buddy, *you bent the knee.'*

128

Joe, in a gesture of sportsmanship, addresses
the parlous state of their drinks. Not that he
needs to collect his thoughts: the cards that he
holds are invincible, both players know it.

'Yes, it's true, I bent the knee. But I also did Sigrid
a kindness . . .' And now they get down to it.

'Look!' he would say, except neither man needs to:
horizoned, the Isle of Drunks, where it always was.

'Seriously, Arthur, is that what you want –
to spend you retirement weeding the onions?
Writing your daily villanelle, your dictionary
poem, your "five things" exercise? Come on,
big guy, that's not you – not even Bardruin's
pride demands that. Do you honestly want
some teenage whizz kid lecturing you on
the expressive fallacy?' 'Stop it, Joe. Please.'
'No, *listen* to me, Arthur. If not for
your own sake then do it for Marigold –
God knows why, but she wants to take care
of you, lucky old goat – you just have to
let her. You're fond of her, aren't you? Okay
then, do it! Sleep and fuck and watch the golf
on television. Laugh at gilded butterflies.
Ordinary human happiness, maestro,
what's so contemptible in that? Who knows,
after your recantation ('more joy in
Heaven' and all that stuff) they might even
let you do a bit teaching – life-writing,
say, at the Pearly Shells – nice little

sinecure, drinking money. But *oh no,
not for Arthur Bardruin!* Bardruin has to
throw all that away for the sake of a poem
that no one else wants. For Christ's sake,
Arthur, get a grip! *Shape up*, citizen!'

The poet, weight slumped over his knees, close-
reads the stains in the bottom of his teacup.
Joes's part is almost discharged. He feels
dreadful about it. 'Look, Arthur, all I'm asking
of you' – trying not to press his advantage too
firmly – 'is keep your head down, think it over,
and think about Marigold, okay? Toss out
a fishing line, work on the suntan. Arthur . . .
can you do that for me?'
       Silence.
         '*Please* . . .
And as for this' – he waves the offending
document – 'there wouldn't be a carbon
stashed around here somewhere? *Scout's
honour?* Okay, then. This stays with me.'

CHAPTER 14

Creature of habit, perverse but compliant,
Frank does his thing in the hamster wheel.
Week after week, from a vast elevation
he watches his rat-sized felonious avatar
finger stalled on the baleful buzzer
steeling itself for the arctic blast.
The silence, he means. His mother's
depression. The bruised yellow snow-cloud
of pain and reproach. The Friday just past,
he explains to Juanita, he found himself
stuck to his seat in the train – rode to the end
and then back to the city – slept for an
hour on a park bench, then had to try
again. 'I'd expected you sooner,' his mother
had said. 'Did you sleep in?' He picks
at a hangnail. The analyst says nothing.

'Did I tell you about when she first became
ill, with the Parkinson's? If that's what it
was . . . I mean, plainly it *was*, and we more
or less knew, but nothing would make her
talk about it. The whole thing was crazy. She

wouldn't touch an instrument (not even now
for her students, they told me); the shaking
was so bad she couldn't hold a glass – and we
all carried on as if nothing was happening.
It was simply impossible to ask what was
wrong. Her friends were indignant; they'd
bail me up: "What's going on with Alice?"
and so on. Like the whole thing was *my* fault.
But why look at me? I mean, they couldn't
talk to her any more than I could!
It isn't just me, do you see what I'm
saying? It's *her*, it's this silence, like
a physical thing, she emits it,
you catch it just by being in the room.

'There was one time with Paula –'
                                    'That's Paula
your ex-wife?'
                    'Right. Just a little bit
later than this; it may be by this time we'd
given it a name. Anyway, Mum came
to stay overnight, I remember it clearly
because it hardly ever happened. Nobody
wanted it, certainly not me. And not Paula,
either – she really couldn't stand her.
But Mum was in town for a show or
something, and we took her out with us, then
back to our flat. We were living upstairs,
which was difficult enough, but somehow
we managed to get her inside. Then what
I remember is switching the lights on,
shutting the kitchen door behind us, and

her getting stuck there, her meds must have
worn off – she locked up. The thing is, though,
we did as well. That was the weird part, Paula
and I, it's as if we were paralysed
just like her. The three of us stood – this is
literally true – we must have been stuck there
for forty-five minutes, acting like all this was
perfectly normal, and we couldn't do a damn
thing about it. We couldn't say, "Alice, can we
help you to bed?" We just stood there, trying
to make small talk like strangers at a party.'

Which is more than his analyst is doing,
thinks Frank, in the silence that follows.
With his eyes closed, he drifts. In moments
like this there's a task he finds restful; he
tries to remember the contents of Juanita's
bookcase. Top shelf, left to right: *Philosophy
in the Bedroom, Bliss and Other Stories,
The Songs of Maldoror, Le Plaisir du
Texte, Inquisiciones, The Aleph, Murphy,
Seminar VII, Four Suit Transfers* –
                                   'Hey,
that's weird,' he hears himself saying, his
eyes springing open, 'this dream, last night. It
just came back, a fragment of it: a voice
that's saying *the rungs are frozen*. Rungs, like
on one of those wire bridges . . . that's right, with
somebody perching on it, a dwarf, or –
I don't know – a troll . . . of course! It's that
story, "The Billy Goats Gruff", do you know it?
It used to scare the living crap out me!

Behind him he seems to hear an intake
of breath . . . he waits for Juanita to speak,
but she doesn't. They hang, for what feels
like a long time, in cavernous silence.
'So, Paula, you're saying' – eventually
it's Juanita who steps in to set them
moving – 'Paula found it just as sticky.
The troll-mother's not just an old wives' tale?'

'Exactly, yes. She froze up the both of us, like
she does anyone who comes within reach.
Except . . . you know, that's not quite true.
There were just a few months – I'd forgotten
this, it can't have been long before she
and I split – where Paula and Alice made
friends. It was all very strange. Paula, I've
probably said this before, she could talk
the hind leg off a donkey, right? Hell, she
could talk the hind leg off a billy goat!
Anyway, just for a while they were close.
It seems kind of unreal now, but it happened:
they chummed up together like a pair of old
phone hags. And somehow Paula coaxed her out.
Hours and hours they'd spend on the phone. Paula
would always have some project – a person,
I mean, like a crush, but not really – and just
for a month or two Alice was it. I'd
hear her turning on the charm, the empathy,
whatever it was, and Mum seemed to talk about
everything: about music, her illness,

the Judge. About widowhood. Christ, they even
talked about sex! Not that I wanted to know,
of course, but Paula told me anyway, how
Mum, when she got ill, was taken in tow
by a lesbian couple, and how much she
liked them, and how, she had said, if her life
had been different . . . I couldn't believe it –
not that in particular – just the sheer
fact of their talking together. Poor thing,
I thought it might blow all her fuses to
find herself suddenly sharing like that.
But then Paula lost interest, or moved
on, whatever . . .'
                    'Your ex-wife refused her.'
'Yes, something like that. Paula's a shedder:
she travels light.'
                    'And took your mother's feelings
lightly?'
            'Well . . .'
                    'So how did you feel about that?'
'Was I hurt, do you mean, on my mother's
behalf? Was I angry? I wouldn't go that far.
It was *my* mother – let's be fair – not hers,
and it wasn't like I was going to
pick up the slack. I'm resentful of Paula
for all sorts of things: for being so
unshakeable, for not having children,
for going on and doing so much
better without me. But no. I was happy
enough while it lasted, but when she
got sick of it I couldn't complain.'

135

'When she got sick of Alice?'

　　　　　　　　　'Look, I hear what
you're saying: she toyed with her feelings. But
damn it all, those feelings aren't my problem!'

'Really?'

　　　　　　　　'Okay, fair enough.' He laughs. 'But
they shouldn't be, that's what I'm saying.
It's parents who make the rules, not kids. I mean,
not that I blame her, but she wrote the playbook.
Dealer's choice, right? *She* taught *me*. So
if I can't talk to her, whose fault is that?
If nobody likes her, if she's so hard to
love, if the nursing staff can't stand
to be in the same room with her, how
can that be down to *me*, for Christ's sake?
I can't make her loveable! There she sits,
propped up in the pillows like some fucking
monument to Suffering Virtue . . .
I'm not going to sign for the package,
that's all there is to it. I'm sorry,
I know this all sounds pretty childish,
it's hard to explain it, even to you.
It's like I must have a receptor
somewhere – not in the brain, in the
base of the spine – and every time she
gawps at me with that hideous, pitiful,
pleading expression I just want to run screaming
out of the room and throw myself under
a train or something. I swear to you, one day
she'll give me that look and I'm going to
put a pillow over her face and – '

'Stop!'

'No, listen, really, I am. I'm going to
put her out of her fucking misery –'

'Stop, I said! For heaven's sake. You can't say
that sort of thing in here.'
'I can't?' The surprise
in his voice is real. 'I thought I just told you
whatever I'm thinking. Isn't that the only rule?
I tell you whatever comes into my head . . .'

'Frank, you just threatened to suffocate someone.'

'What? No . . . you're *serious*?'
'. . .'
'You can't be.
Oh, come on Juanita, get real. This is just nuts – I was
mouthing off. Honestly, you don't imagine
I'm literally going to kill my mother?'

'Why not . . . ? Look, we've talked about this.
It's not about what I imagine, it's about
what you say. You tell me you're thinking of
smothering someone. You describe how you'll
do it. You insist that I listen. And that's
what I do, because that's why I'm here.
I'm paying attention. That's my job.'

Frank swings around on the couch, plants
both feet on the floor. 'Come on, Juanita,
you're not being straight with me. Aren't we both
talking about something else?'

137

'Are we? I'm just trying
to listen.' Scribbling away – even now –
on her notepad. 'It's your session, Frank.
I just follow your lead –'
                                  'Oh, for crying out loud!'
'You're right, though. We seem to be done.'

Juanita, still clutching her writing pad, stands.
She strides to the door, which she opens, then
shuts again.
                    'Frank, you need to promise me
something. You won't leave the island. You won't
see your mother . . .'
                                  '. . .'
                                  'I'm going to interpret
your silence as "yes". Am I right . . . ?
Then I'll see you on Monday. Goodbye Frank.'

                              ✄

'Holá Pancho!' The greeting is Wanda's, but Frank's
had enough of things Spanish for one morning.
He lets her slip by with her armload of blankets
as he makes for the shade of a Moreton Bay fig.
The high-water dazzle is hard on his eyes;
he feels anxious, confused; he's really not well.
This much, however, is clear as daylight:
right now he needs to find Slippery Bob.

CHAPTER 15

At the best of times, if Marigold's honest,
Saturday mornings are a bit of a chore.
She's not an alarm-clock kind of girl.
And this morning is not, by any means,
the best of times. But the market's a duty
she always steps up for, come hell or high
water or miserable hangover – thank
you Joe Bravo, who came by last night with
the news about Arthur, and the time-honoured
remedy. Hangovers don't get better
with age; nor do hard drinkers, it seems, become
more sensible. This one, however, is nothing
if not gritty: she chokes down her painkillers,
showers, and starts loading the vehicle.

At the market she hangs up a gaudy shingle
MARIGOLD INGLE, APOTHECARY
and lays out her menu of potions and lotions,
the avant-garde face scrubs, the weedy
specifics and tonics. The customers
who come trickling by are a small but
dependable flock, not difficult to please.

Brightening her morning – a case in point –
the good-natured advent of Constable
Dave. 'I thought you looked poorly so
I brought you a pancake.' 'Dave, you're
a credit to the uniform.' Coffee as well.
Easy to please because he just likes to
hang, and yet Dave has his sorrows:
a daughter who refuses to eat. 'You
poor man,' says Marigold, 'I wish there was
something . . . I'm sorry, mate, it's out of my
league. This stuff' – she gestures – 'it's
all well and good, but it isn't for what ails
your daughter. Will you talk to Juanita?'
The lawman looks pained. 'Look, I know what
you're thinking, but – hang on, excuse me . . .

Bridget! Where the hell have you been?'

The truth is, the pair haven't seen one another
since Shady Grove, two weeks ago.
                              'Dave, would
you mind? We girls have to talk. Could you
sit with the shop for an hour or so?'
                              He hesitates.
'Oh, *that*. Don't worry, you won't have to
sell any drugs. I've not harvested yet.'

⨺

The stallholders' offerings cover it
all, from the fabulous to the frankly
deplorable: from vintage grubby magazines

to barbecue aprons with amusing designs;
from June Te Patu's feathered lures
to the polished gravels and macramé plant
hangers, dreamcatchers, fridge magnets,
artisan breadboards, handcrafted
trinkets from the sweatshops of Asia.
Jugglers and strummers, palmists and face
painters, eagerly entertain young and old,
while newfangled juices and sizzling meats
replenish their target constituencies.

In tune with this scurfy inclusiveness
is the embassy maintained by the Farm –
bring the family, folks, there's something
for everyone! Sigrid's on deck,
the presentable face, with her on-the-spot
blood-sugar readings and her HRT
goodie bags. Willow pushes massage oils
with suspiciously Kama Sutric names,
while at the neighbouring table Wanda
retails shamefully over-priced yoga
wear; also bolsters, mats and souvenir tea
towels inscribed with adagia from Mr
Iyengar: 'Unhook the senses and bend
inward'; 'Yoga is the teacher of yoga';
'If you can get your armpit open you'll
never be depressed again!'
                                        And not
forgetting the poetry clinic: on duty this
fine autumn morning, Justin Anodyne.
A well-mannered young man, Justin is glad
to peruse your offerings while you wait

and send you away with encouraging
words and a flyer describing the new
season's programme. You might also pick up
a pamphlet or two: 'Seven Habits of
Successful Authors' or that A6 tri-
fold masterpiece, 'Poetry without Tears'.
Again, you can browse – better still,
purchase – the works of the faculty themselves:
Justin's prize-winning *Charm School Eclogues*;
Harriet's latest, the chapbook *Weft*; and last
Xmas stocking season's breakout sensation
The Christian Bogdanovic Method, by Christian
Bogdanovic. But this morning is quiet.
Justin flicks though a Frank Miller, gossips
with Wanda, plays on his phone. When all else
fails he opens his laptop and skims through
the document he drafted last night, 'Judge's
Report: The Dickinson Prize', before pasting
it into a message to Captain Blood.

✄

'Do you mind if we drive somewhere?'
Bridget moves hurriedly, Marigold trailing,
between the parked cars. 'Too many people.
I'm not really, you know. . .' They climb into
Bridget's station wagon. A mile or so beyond
Shady Grove is the track to the beachfront
at Raupo Bay. At low tide the estuary
breathes and gurgles: worm tracks, crab holes
drilled in the mud. They cross the boardwalk, out
to the beach, to the sand, with its oily

glaze and its pimpling of cockle shells.

'I'm sorry to bring you way out here. Will
Dave be okay? It feels so much better.'
Bridget, as they get ready to walk, takes out
a packet of cigarettes, lights one –
                                        '*Really . . . ?*'
The pair exchange speaking looks. Then: 'Oh Christ,
Bridget, what the hell am I thinking? I'm sorry.'
'It's okay.'
            'No.'
                    'But it is. Truly, there wasn't
a thing you could do. Sooner or later – I was, like,
on a mission, you see? – I was always going to
fuck myself up. But I'm clean again now.'
'You've talked to Juanita?'
                                'Of course I have.'
                                            'About –'
'Frank?'
            'Who's her patient!'
                                'Marigold, stop!
It's a clusterfuck. What do you want me to say?'

Which isn't a question. But still, it's worth
asking: what *does* she want to hear, Marigold
wonders? The gory details? (Honestly, no.)
An explanation? (But what's the point?)
Forgiveness, then? (Of course – as ever –
except that it isn't in anyone's gift.)

They walk in a not very comfortable silence.

It's Bridget who finally rescues them.

'You want to know the very worst thing
about meth?'
        'Of course.'
           'It's a gateway drug for
tobacco.'
      'Ha-bloody-ha, you skank!' says
Marigold, latching hold of the other's arm –
and Bridget pulling up, turning towards her,
as Marigold cradles the back of her head.
'Just so you know – if I ever had to watch
you go back to using, it would ruin my life.'
It's crude, but she doesn't know how else to say it.
She mimes the gentlest Liverpool kiss.

Across the flats, in the middle distance,
shellfish gatherers stoop and fossick, the light
in their buckets like plastic sails, the white
of their gumboots bright against the muddy
grey creek. Boof! Boof! cries a happy dog
as it chases a seagull down the spit
towing a wake of delighted kids
who scold that *bad dog* furiously.

'Well . . .' says Bridget, turning for home –
it's time to get back, and they've run out of
beach – 'that's me sorted, but what about you?
What are *you* so hungover about?' Marigold
groans. Where on earth to begin? Really,
she'd rather not go there at all. Or so
she protests – but then, once she gets started,

144

it turns out she wants to talk loud and long,
and to call down a plague on the poetry
police, and to blacken the name of her
sequestered lover, and to curse his attachment
to his childish effusions, and to curse
her own childish attachment *to him.*
And that she even wants to smoke one of
Bridget's fags – her first in, say, ten years or
more – *so who's lost the plot now?*

                    'The question,'
says Bridget, 'have I got this right – the question
is, will Arthur put it aside? And Joe
reckons *maybe.'*

           'Or maybe not.'

                    'In which case
the man must be nuts.'

              'But he is! That's the point.'
They arrive at the car. Bridget turns the ignition;
then, pausing a moment, considering,
switches it off.

           'I'm not sure,' she says, 'but
it's possible – maybe – there's something Juanita
told me about. She *shouldn't* have told me –
it's my fault entirely, it's kind of fucked up –
but it might almost work. If I talked it through
with her, would that be okay? I've been such a
trial to you, sweetheart. I'd so like to help!'

⚔

Abigail Dorothy (Dottie) Dickinson
came to her calling late in life. Not that she

lacked the pedigree: Nantucket Dickinsons
have hobnobbed with Cabots and Lowells
and what-have-you since time immemorial.
But poetry failed to speak to her until
her eightieth year, in the Pearly Shells
Rest Home. It was there, on the other side
of the world, where she'd finally followed
her only son – the boy she christened Dyer
John, but known to us as Captain Blood – that
the old lady heard and fell under the spell of
a feisty young poetry instructor
named Harriet Whitbread. The folio
Dottie would eventually write under
Harriet's guidance at the BPWF
divided its in-house and external readers
(the phrase 'senile dementia' was redacted
from the final report). But her supervisor
was in no doubt: her manuscript was
'the austere map of a voyage into post-semic
alterity'. And even if Harriet's publisher
demurred – the 'time' being 'not quite right' –
the poet left behind her a goodly sum and
a dutifully soft-hearted sole legatee.
'Captain, my captain!' as Justin now
greets him, the same son and heir sidling up
to his stall. Under his arm is a thick roll
of posters which the mild-mannered skipper
unfurls with a flourish. 'Look at these beauties!'
In fact, they're quite plain. It's the message they
carry that quickens the pulse. The SWORDFISH CLUB
where THE PEN IS MIGHTIER hosts its annual
GALA READING. Hear the Island's BEST

YOUNG POETS! With emcee CAPTAIN BLOOD.
Plus OPEN MIC!!! And announcing the winner of
this year's DOROTHY DICKINSON PRIZE.

'Great work, Skipper,' enthuses Justin. 'Give us
a dozen, we'll paste them around. Did you get
my report?'
      'Damn right I did! And I tell you,
we're going to have a whale of a time. My
favourite night of the year, did I say that?
Dear old Moms. It would make her so proud!'

CHAPTER 16

Drop thy pipe, thy happy pipe, hums a folksy
Frank. It's Monday morning. Breakfast
having taken a powdered form, he's as ready
as he's ever going to be to front up to Juanita.

As usual, the door opens silently.

When he makes for his customary place
on the couch, however, the analyst
heads him off.
   'This is not psychotherapy,
Frank. It's a housekeeping session. We won't be
long.'
   Shooing him into a straight-backed chair
she takes up station at her writing desk. Shy of
her gaze, he contemplates a dog-eared manilla
folder with (he guesses) his name on it.

'The question,' she says, in a formal tone,
'is safety. Can we agree about that?'

'It all depends,' says Frank.

'On what?'
                                    'On whose.'
'Well, yours, for one. And mine. And your mother's,
of course. As you'll understand, I am
now obliged to speak with her.'
                              'You *what?*'
'It's that, or law enforcement. Whichever
you like. It's known as "duty to warn".'

Frank glares back at her, open-mouthed,
aware of the blood-flush storming his features.

'Whatever happened to trust?' he manages.
'What if I said that the question was *betrayal?*'

Juanita looks back at him levelly.

'I'd say that was an interesting turn of
phrase, given whom you were speaking to.'

'Okay! So now we're getting warmer.'
                                    'Really?
What of your poor, cold mother?'
                                    'Oh, come on,
we can drop that, can't we? Let's talk about
what's really happening. We both know
the mother thing's just an excuse.'
                                    'I know what your
words tell me, Frank. All the rest is imaginary.'

Yeah, whatever. Lacanian squid-ink.
Frank's morning buzz is beginning to fray,

his eyes are scratchy. It makes him reckless:
'Okay, so what about Bridget then?'

He holds his breath, but the analyst's mask
remains imperturbably in place.

'Here's what you don't seem to understand, Frank.
Bridget is real: she's a human person.
Just like the girl with the plastic bag over
her face is real –'
                    'Her name is Sophie.'

'Sophie is real, which is why she liked you.'

'And why I felt bad – why I told you
about it. But, truly, does that make me so
confused that you seriously think I'm going to
strangle my mother? Come on, be honest.'

'Honest, you want? Well how about this:
can you honestly say that we wouldn't be safer –
your mother, Sophie, Bridget, me – that we'd
not all be safer with Frank off the streets?'

Adjudging the question rhetorical
he keeps his own counsel . . . such as it is,
for he only half-hears her. Frank never
sat in this chair before and his gaze
has been trapped by the image behind her,
an aerial vista of vice-toned Miami,
Christo's islands lit up in their hot
pink skirts. Of course, he thinks, with an inward

150

sigh, the usual analytic bunk, and yet –

'There's also the patient's safety, Frank,
I need to be mindful of that.
The drugs, I mean – where's all that going?
Does Frank have another rehab in him?'

The unsafe patient shrugs his shoulders.

'Come on, you can do better than that!
This doesn't have to end in tears. You're
not a bad person, I think – you pretend . . .'

But he's really not listening. He's worlds away,
in the turquoise sea-haze of Biscayne Bay
where a fleet of flamingo-liveried islands
sets sail into a past that used to feel like
a future. He's digging it now, its ephemeral
joy: the image is achingly beautiful.
What a heart-breaking world we imagined once, what
a sumptuous palette we gave up the use of . . .

'So, here's what I need you to do for me, Frank.
I need you to go out to Shady Grove
and talk to Bridget. *Listen* to her.
She has a suggestion to make. I think
it may help us both.'
                          Is Frank perplexed?
Demonstrably, though he's smart enough
not to seek clarification. And is he
intrigued? A little, perhaps, though it
can't be a playdate, they're well beyond that.

Most of all, Frank is flattening out.
He wants to get home to his happy pipe.

Rising, Juanita extends her hand. They shake
and he thanks her. For what, he has no idea.

CHAPTER 17

'Hi, I'm Bridget. I'm an addict.'

Hi, Bridget.

'Thanks for asking me to share. I don't feel
great, I'm kind of nervous – shamed, I
guess, is how I feel – so thank you for letting
me speak before I run out of courage.
Not that anyone's going to judge me,
I realise that. We've all been through it.
I've been in your place often enough, watching
one of us crawl back in here, dragging their
arse along the floor. The embarrassment
thing – I get this – it's in my own head.
So thank you for all the hugs and so on. I'm
a grateful addict. I'm in the right place.
And I do know it's possible to leave this
room and not ever have to use drugs again.

'Anyway, first thing, I just have to say it, three
little words – little big words. I PICKED UP.
Seven years clean, and I went out and

blew it. But that's this disease, right? – it's
always just an arm's length away. It could
have been worse, it was just a few days;
I've not lost my job, which is lucky, and
my partner's been great. In spite of the fact
that I seem to have messed up her life even
more than mine – as we do, because once we
start using then of course everything's
all about us. Well, now it really *is*
about me: it's all my shit, it's no one
else's, and somehow I have to clean it up.

'You know that thing we like to say
about how you pick up *before* you pick up?
It always makes me think of the person
who got me clean the second time round
and became my sponsor, saved my life –
she'd say that all the time, except I
never quite got it. Well, guess what? It's true.
It couldn't be simpler. Just before Christmas
I was seven years clean. So what did
I do? I marked it by not showing up.
What the fuck, I mean how dumb is that,
to celebrate your birthday by acting out?
I guess it was partly about my dad.
Actually, I *know* it was – and that's the thing,
I loved him, right, but I'm always making
excuses for him. He had this disease
as well – an alcoholic, a whisky drinker,
he'd nibble away from dawn till dusk.
He worked as a sales rep, travelled a lot,
and he'd drink on the road – I mean, *literally* –

driving the company station wagon
with a bottle of spirits between his knees.
Now and then if Mum was busy I'd go
out with him for a day or two and on
one of those trips he rolled the car. You can
guess what my mother thought about that!
I wasn't hurt, but that was it: I never
went with him again. But also, by that
time the marriage was over. I never
really knew when it ended, the trips just
got longer. A year or two later he
drove himself into a bridge stanchion.
My mother was a whole different
story, she didn't use anything. Dad
was musical, sentimental, he made
a big deal of his folks being Irish.
Mum was scraped back, rational, disciplined,
called herself a scientist. I'm sorry,
I should say she *was* a scientist, she
worked as a radiographer. But also,
she prided herself on that, on her
logical mind, her efficiency, that
kind of thing. You wouldn't say she was
warm exactly. She got things done, though,
she took care of us. And then she got cancer –
a radiographer! – what's that about, where's
the science in that? Excuse me, I'm rambling,
my head's a bit wrecked . . . but I'll get there,
just give me moment. Bear with me . . .

'Back when Mum was still alive, I didn't
really think of myself as "using". Sure,

155

there was booze, the odd bit of weed, but
I was a student, you know, it was just
what you did. Then the summer she died
I came up to the island. A girlfriend
from film school – a "friend", to be clear,
though it's true she was the first chick I
ever tried to sleep with . . . anyway, her
family had a holiday place, one of those
baches off the end of the causeway, and
she brought me up here, the very first time.
Now, some of you guys will remember this,
it was back when there was all that coke.
I fetched up here at the dead right moment –
dead *wrong* moment – and, honestly,
that was that. The first time I did it
all I could think was: "Man, I'm in love!"
With coke, I mean. I was so starving
hungry, so empty, so lost. There was
quite a good scene happening, nice young guys,
we'd party with the Gaucho Airways crowd,
and I had a bit of money that my mother had
left me, not a great deal, but it was enough
to get me well and truly wrecked. Needless
to say, it was the end of Film School. Jane
went back – she's in Sydney now, she's
worked on some films – but I wasn't going
anywhere. The money ran out, but there was
plenty of work, I was doing two jobs (it was
no sweat – that fabulous coke!). For a year
or two it was really great; in some ways
I don't entirely regret it. And I guess I got
lucky, because what happened then – again,

you might remember this – is the powder
dried up. And I still had enough sense, just,
to get back home and do my first rehab.

'But you know what it's like when you're too
young for it. At this stage I was twenty-five.
I got out of Nazareth, I came in the rooms,
and I knew that my life was unmanageable.
But somehow I didn't quite believe it.
Deep down I didn't really *want* it. Mostly
I wanted to be clean so I could use again.

'I'm sorry if I'm telling you the story of
my life, which I realise is not what you
came here for, but I have to describe this
next bit. I met this guy. He was a few
years older, he seemed pretty smart,
in fact he *was* smart, and funny, and so on.
Also – excuse the oversharing but
I have to say this – he was crash-hot
in bed. Which was new, in a way. I mean,
I'd had lots of sex, I guess I'd maybe
had too much; I liked it, just never
really "got" it. But this was all different;
to tell the truth he pretty much taught me.
Like I was saying, I'd come out of rehab,
and I was kind of in the rooms, except
I wasn't, if you know what I mean.
I was drinking a little; it seemed a waste
not to, the whole thing was all so
romantic, of course I was going to drink.
And – guess what? – this guy just so happened

to be a user. So . . . there we were,
I hate to say it, but there we were having
all this sex, and he asked if I'd
ever done it on meth. (Like, you
think this is good? You've got no idea!)
I'm oversharing again, I'm sorry, but
I need to remind myself what happened
next. Not that you can't guess already, it's
not rocket science. First up, it blew me
away. I mean totally. Just like the first
time round with coke, falling in love all over
again, with the drug, and with the guy as well.
It's an honest programme, I have to add that bit.
In some ways at least, he was good for me.
Reckless, I guess, and a bit self-obsessed,
but so was I, so what the hell? The sight
of a skinny-looking boy with a meth pipe
I have to say still turns the knees to jelly.
Oh dear! Anyway, it all went bad – who
would have guessed? – it turned to shit, the fun
tapered off and the rest was just using . . .
more and more, and the stuff that goes with it,
stuff that I wouldn't have dreamed of doing:
stealing, slinging, selling sex. From best sex
to worst – it took eighteen months – awful,
dreary, degrading stuff. Turning tricks
in the backs of cars. Utter trash. I'll
tell you what – *I* wouldn't have fucked me.

'Jesus Christ, I'm rabbiting on. I don't
think I've ever shared for such a long time.
And you're getting the crap, not the clean-up,

but right now *that's me*. It just feels so dumb
to be back here again, picking up this
stupid white key tag. I'm sorry, do you mind . . . ?'

You're good, Bridget.
Go for it.
Kei te pai.

'Okay. So that was a really low moment,
"gift of desperation" stuff. And here, looking
back, is where I first got the message. I've
been thinking a lot about Marama:
she was the person I mentioned before who
scraped me up off the footpath and got me
cleaned up again. I went back to Nazareth,
did another rehab, then Marama
frog-marched me into the rooms.
I lived with her, she became my sponsor,
she held my hand at Social Welfare.
And slowly I started to get the programme.
We went through the steps, and I saw what it
might mean to stop living so absolutely *for me*.
I discovered there was something more powerful
than drugs. And I learned what we all have to learn
in these rooms: that there's a better way to live
and that we can't do it alone. Oh damn,
now I'm tearing up, it always happens
when I talk about this; she saved my life,
no question about it, and now she's not
here: she went out and never got back.
She'd been clean for ever – like, fifteen years –
and that's what can happen, to anyone; she

picked up, and now she's gone. What would she
say to me, I wonder? Not something clever.
Just, get your skinny arse back in the chair!

'So Marama taught me that I couldn't
be "cured" but I could have an altogether
different life. And that's when I came back
up here, to the island, which sounds kind of
dumb after all that had happened – and even
more when the person I came up to stay with
had been a big part of my using. Strange
as it sounds, though, I knew I could trust her.
She loved me, she mothered me, really.
Still does. And that's when I finally
began to grow up. I learned how to eat
and to sleep and keep healthy. And then
I met my partner, which was a total
revelation; honest to God, I had no
idea, but then I met the right person
and I thought: "Wow, *this* is better than
drugs!" I was right, it still is, if I could
only remember. It was all just so
different, and I don't mean the sex – well,
I do, but not *just* that – I mean the whole
thing. Because mostly it wasn't about
that at all: it was more about respect, or
I guess *self*-respect, self-acceptance. I
think back to when I was fourteen or so –
the women here know what I'm talking about –
overnight, men were completely different,
they're looking at you like a piece of meat.
You think, Jesus, what's happening? It takes

a while to sink in, or at least that's how
it was for me. And sometimes, sure, if
I'm honest about it, I don't mind
being a piece of meat. But not all the time,
right? It's not who I am, I don't need it
printed on a business card. *Occupation:
piece of meat*. Fuck you, Jack! You know?
And that's the thing: even when I don't deserve
it, she still treats me like I've got a brain.

'Anyway, that's how I really got well.
I came to the island, I found my sweetheart,
I found my houseboat, I got a good job.
And ever since then I've been here in the rooms:
I'm an addict, I know, but I've got a good
programme; I've learned how to do the suggested
things. And yet look at me: here I am,
two days clean – this fucking disease, man!
All it takes, you turn your back for a minute . . .

'Except that's not quite true. It was more than
a minute – you pick up before you pick up,
like I said. I mentioned that birthday I didn't
show up for. So what's happening there?
Well, here's what I think: I was looking
for attention – would anyone miss me,
was anyone going to come and find me?
That's what it felt like, a plea to be noticed,
addressed to myself – I could hear it – but
I didn't *want* to hear it. Because what
I really wanted was to get fucked up.
It goes that way when things are good: it's like,

life's *too good*, too stable. Where's the chaos?
My girlfriend's kind of a serious person –
she's an intellectual, incredibly
smart – but I'm not, really. Not like that.
Juanita's a healer, that's her job, but
me, it's like sometimes I just want to
wreck something. I think to myself, I'm
too young to be clean, I deserve to . . .
for Christ's sake, I'm going to be forty! It's
just like we say at the start of each meeting:
*we had to have something different
and we thought we'd found it in drugs.*

'And sex, I guess. It's like I was saying,
show me a skinny-looking boy with a
a crack pipe . . . and what's *really* stupid, I
saw it coming, I'd had half an eye on
this guy for a while – I kidded myself
that I didn't, but I did – it could hardly
have been more inevitable. I cheated
with drugs. I cheated with sex. And now,
if I'm not really careful, I could lose
my relationship. It isn't so much that
I slept with someone – it's not just the fact
that I picked up, either – the thing is, I've
brought that crap into her life, and her work,
and now she has to sort it all out. I'm
worried that *she* might have stuffed up now.
I can't share about it, of course, but it's
bad: in her line of work this is
serious shit, and if she's got it wrong
then it's all on me. Me and this fucking

disease. I mean, addicts, who needs us?

'I'm sorry, this has truly been the crappiest
sharing. Sharing the mess, not the message!
But there *is* a message here. At least for me.
It's plain as daylight: like we always say,
it's a simple programme. I'm just going
to have to get over my shame, get my arse
in the seat, do the next right thing: a shit-
load of meetings, a shitload of stepwork,
a whole lot of showing up for my own
recovery. And a heap of amends, and trying
to be a good partner. Today I don't
have to use drugs. Thanks for letting me share.'

CHAPTER 18

All the world loves a Poetry Reading
and the good folks of Rock Oyster Island
are no different. It's a testing drive
out to Bluewater Cove – a narrow, dusty
dry-weather road – but the parking lot at
the Swordfish Club tonight is bursting
at the seams: SUVs and Commer vans,
utes and quadbikes, Harley three-wheelers
spill out along the grassy verge ('For Christ's
sake,' a biker advises, 'look out where
yr going!'). In the lounge bar, poetry
enthusiasts are hanging from the rafters.
Air-kissing socialites and high-fiving
hipsters, dope fiends and olive growers
scrummage without prejudice.
Wiki Laulala behind the beer taps
has to shout simply to make herself heard.

For Caitlin Zinger, who edits the Arts &
Society page for the *Island Times*, it's
a night at the office (little does she know
she's about to be handed the year's biggest

story). For three-term mayor Leilani Jones
it's all about 'the magic of the spoken word.
We're a world-class Island of Poetry!'
she affirms into Caitlin's dictaphone.
Everyone wants their picture taken for
the weekly photo-spread 'Frocks on the Rock'.
What Caitlin would like is a comment from
Sigrid. 'There's talk going round that
the poetry programme up at the Farm might be –'
'What – are you kidding? *The outlook for*
poetry in our island community has never
been brighter. Okay? You can quote me.'

A dozen creative-writing students
mingle in front of the makeshift stage
where Caitlin has rounded them up for a photo.
It's no easy feat: they are sugar-crazed,
feverish, skittery. And why not? The evening
is all about them. Tonight they officially
graduate: they have five minutes each at
the podium to announce their arrival
in the poetry workforce. All afternoon
the helipad has been welcoming their
bashful progenitors, bent low, cowed
by the rotor blast and weighed down with gifts
for their teachers. The stakes are not trivial.

Down go the house lights. Up steps Captain Blood.
A mihi, some well-chosen lines from his
mother, some house-keeping notes, then it's straight

down to business: 'Ladies and gentlemen,
Islanders all' – he opens his arms
magnanimously – 'the future of poetry
begins right here, and as you're about
to discover, it's in excellent hands.'

The evening's first reader is William Chang.
Is he nervous? Of course. But you'd hardly
believe it. Astonishing, really, how far
he's come, riffing his way through a sly
introduction, then knocking them dead with
a crafty pantoum whose pay-off line reads:
'What does that even *mean*?' He spins it out
drily, to riotous cheers, descends from
the stage to low fives from his colleaguely
classmates. Out in the audience Caitlin
makes notes on her phone. As the season's new
talents take their turn to exhibit, she's
pleased to confirm it's a vintage crop.
Luminous detail, she thumbs in the dark.
Heart-blasting metaphors. Limber imaginings.
Honeyed word-music that melts in the mouth!
Calisthenic syntax that trips off the tongue!

In due course only one remains, and to
no one's surprise it's Mei-Lin Chin. Justin's
citation for the Dickinson Prize (from which
the Captain quotes liberally) makes
reference to 'footwork' and 'technical dazzle',
to 'bricolage', 'arbitrage', 'frottage' and
'playing on all the staves'. Insouciantly
the young woman strides to the podium.

166

Her heels are approximately six inches
tall, i.e. roughly the length of the miniskirt
(in violet leather) which rides at the trot
above fishnets of cunningly distressed
design. Adjusting the mic stand, she peeks out
from under her bangs. She'd just like to say
how humbling it's been to share this course
with such awesome talent. The prize is for
all of them (cheers, kia oras.) She is going to
read one poem only. She wrote it today.
It isn't quite finished, she begs their indulgence,
it's called: 'What the Fuck Are You Looking At?'

🗡

'How are you doing, my old friend? It's almost
time.'
          Arthur Bardruin tosses away
his stumpy cigar butt; it dies with a hiss.
He pushes himself to his feet and they
pad down the jetty. Above them, a flight
of wooden steps and the club-house
strung with fairy lights, the babble
of tipsy poetry lovers hanging
outside in the intermission, smoking
and gossiping. Joe puts an arm around
Bardruin's shoulder. 'I talked to Marigold,'
he says. 'She understands about tonight.
She'll expect you round lunchtime tomorrow.
I promised you'll be there.' Bardruin
takes out a silver hipflask, drinks, then
shakes it reproachfully. 'Don't worry,'

Joe says, 'there's more in the vehicle. But
easy does it, brother. We need you on song.'

The carcass hangs from a gallows at
the head of the dock. A night light affixed
to a nearby packing shed casts it half
in light and half in gloom. Slate-grey
belly, peunumbral back, its lilacs
and blues have drained back to the ocean;
the mouth has been gaffer-taped to the bill.
On the flat of its flank, in crisp white paint,
its captors have stencilled its epitaph:

165 kg.

The two men stare at it wordlessly. Then:
'Come on Arthur,' Joe says gently. 'You've
made the right decision. Let's get it over with.'

⚔

Open mic? I hear you shudder, O fastidious
reader – but not so fast! Blackboard readings,
island-style, are not what the mainlander
might imagine. Not with Captain Blood at
the helm; not with the Terrible Triplets
reading; not with every last space in the line-up
spoken for hours ahead of time. The local punters
expect no less: they take their poetry
seriously, and as they chew over
the evening's list the room comes alive with
a knowledgeable buzz. Everyone
knows Stockcar Derek and his endlessly
iterating 'Ford Fourteeners'. They've all

heard Wanda channelling Rumi, and the
Triplets, of course, of whom many harbour
quite firm opinions. Not till they come to
the final two names on the blackboard does
anything catch them off-guard. *Anyone know
who this 'Arthur' is?* The question passes
from row to row. The Captain's preamble
leaves no one the wiser:
                              'I'm going to let
our second-last reader introduce himself . . .'

At the head of the phalanx steps June Te Patu
with Sigrid and Willow on either arm;
behind the women, Constable Dave,
Manfred, Joe and Koro Bill. And the tall
gangly figure whose features emerge as
they enter the stage lights? That must be
'Arthur'. Koro and Joe, each clasping an
elbow, shepherd him to the microphone.

Front row, centre, Christian Bogdanovic,
gripping the holster he wears on a shoulder-strap,
leaps to his feet. *E noho!* says Koro.
Grudgingly Christian resumes his seat.
Joe mutters something in the tall figure's
ear, then retires to stand watch with
the others at the rear of the stage.

᚛

'Citizens, punters, poetry lovers –
I beg your attention. I won't be long. *It is*

closing time in the gardens of the West and . . .
something, something, something . . . never mind.

'I speak tonight on behalf of the late poet
Arthur Bardruin. "Late" as in "former",
"erstwhile", "ex-". He whom we used to
refer to as. Despite what you may have
heard, Bardruin, Arthur, man in the street,
is in rude good health. Not so, however,
his spectral other – *Bardruin, now*
former poet. It is time for his song.'

Arthur pauses, swaying a little,
steadies himself at the lectern and pats down
his pockets. What's this? Ah! his resupplied
flask (he celebrates with a temperate slug).
And this? A soiled page of script. With studied
deliberation he palms it flat.
Lastly, the question of reading glasses,
a handkerchief to mop the brow, a turning
right-side-up of the page, a moment's
silent, prayer-like pause, and then –

'Arthur Bardruin – sometime author –
upright, sober and uncoerced – wishes to make
known the following facts and particulars.
(1) That, as of the moment of writing,
he surrenders all claim to the office of
Poet. He shall no longer write, read, recite,
publish or otherwise disseminate
any canto, sutra, stanza, strophe or
fragment of poetic verse. (2) That

170

he likewise surrenders all claim to
the baubles of poetic reputation.
(3) Concerning those poetic works
already at large in the public domain, that
he offers them, with sincere contrition,
as a cautionary model: *go forth
and do otherwise*. (4) Pursuant to
the previous item (younger listeners
please take note), that the author of these
regrettable texts hereby repudiates
the following: poverty; alcohol;
Zen meditation; standing outside in
electrical storms; cloudy trophies;
stovepipe trousers; the deregulation
of the senses; the works of Freud; the *au
dela*; miasmas; vapours; velvet jackets;
the works of Shelley; the body electric;
the body vehicular; pure strains of
unpremeditated art; the gem-like
flame; the procreant urge; cigarettes;
heroin; moonlight; dharma; the axe
for the frozen sea inside us; and
emotion re-cathected in senility.

'He accepts that the judgement of History
is final and that no correspondence
will be entered into. He hopes you will
enjoy your evening and drive home safely.'

In the general brouhaha that follows
(the hugs and kisses and shoulder-patting,
the audience babble and wild surmise,
the mass rendition of 'Whakaaria Mai')
the room is swept up almost entirely.

Almost? Not so the Terrible Triplets
(Christian slumps in his chair with a face like
thunder). Certainly not Caitlin Zinger,
scribbling at furious pace on her phone.

And not the figure in the pork-pie hat
who sits unnoticed at the back of the room
immersed in a somehow unbreachable
solitude, drumming his fingers on a manuscript.

'Ladies and gentlemen, if I may' –
Captain Blood resuming the mic
as the Bardruin whānau relinquish
the stage and file out, chattering
among themselves – 'as our final reader tonight,
a brand new voice. If you've heard him before
it was never like this! For the first time
ever at the Swordfish Club, would you please
make warmly welcome Mr Frank Hortune!'

✄

Frank feels the warmth of the spots, and yet it's
all unfamiliar. Where's the piano to
hide behind when you need it? He straightens
his script on the lectern. 'Thank you, Skipper.

Thank you everyone. This is all new,'
he begins, 'as the Captain just told you.
Somehow or other, I've written a poem.
Or is it a story? I'm not quite sure.
But a publisher's seen it . . .'

                  He trails off,
arrested, mid-sentence, as Harriet Whitbread,
reaching an arm through the curtain of stage
glare, sets down a winking mobile phone.
She sinks once again through the brightness.
Frank clears his throat.

             'I'd like, if I may,
to read the first few pages, the opening
chapter. (Perhaps it's a novel!) You'll have to
bear with me, I'm a little bit nervous.'

And, hesitantly, he begins to read:

How much Manfred Singleton can see is
subject to dispute . . .

'A picaresque tale of the South Pacific,'
as Caitlin will put it in Monday's edition
('Hortune's poem, while apparently frivolous,
kept his listeners mildly amused'). But
that's just a sidebar – Caitlin's no critic –
her kind of story is what happens next:
as the reading concludes, as the house lights
come up, as Frank, to a sprinkling of
applause, descends from the stage to be greeted by
Christian with taser and plastic flexicuffs.

It isn't straightforward for Arthur to
locate the vehicle. But when he does
the cab's unlocked and the bottle of Famous
Grouse is where Joe left it. What's more, it's
almost two-thirds full. He lowers it
an inch. It's been a trying evening.

Where the carpark ends there's a bench with
a view of the cove. But someone else has the same
idea, he discovers; she offers her hand
in greeting. 'You must be the former poet.
Arthur, yes?' 'And you're . . . Jacinta!' 'Almost.
I'm Juanita.' 'Yes, of course you are. Let's
drink to that! We're almost family, after all –
I mean, your being the mother of Chuck . . .'
'Of whom?' 'Of my new friend Chuck. Don't worry,
Marigold's told me all about it.' 'Sorry?'
'About how you had to lose him, the patients
and everything, spreading gossip.'
                                        'Arthur –'
the analyst pauses, appears to consider.
'Listen, I'm not sure what Marigold told you
but I don't know that bird from Adam. I'm sorry,
I don't like to spoil a good story, but the day
I arrived Señor Chuckles was already with her.'

'Bardruin! Who are you annoying? Is that
you, Nita?' 'It's okay, Joe. Arthur and I

174

are just getting acquainted. Clearing up
a few misconceptions. Aren't we Arthur?'
'Professor Joe,' the ex-poet slurs, have you met
Jacinda?' Juanita laughs. They shuffle
along and Joe collapses thankfully.

'So that's where you've got to!'
                                    The voice
is Bridget's, climbing the steps from the dock
to join them. Settling herself on Juanita's
knee, she slips an arm around her neck.

'It's all right, sweetheart, honestly. It wasn't you
who crossed the line – no, just listen' – stopping
Juanita's lips with a finger – 'Frank's okay.
He's safe from his mother. And he gets to
clean up.'
              'I'm not so sure . . .'
                                    'But I am.
Trust me. What Frank needs is to make amends.
Just like your lover needs to make to you.'

Bardruin, killing the Famous Grouse,
declares in an elegiac tone: 'How Blest
Are Ye Whose Toils Are Ended.' The empty
comes to rest gently in the spongy grass.

'Fine words, those, from a fine ex-poet,'
says Joe. He musses the ex-poet's curls.
'Come on, Arthur, you old disgrace.
It's time we got you home.'

CODA

To Joe's surprise, the garden shed appears
not greatly the worse for wear. It's almost
tidy. The floor's been swept, the cot and card
table folded away. Outside, the most
recent cohort of empties stand to attention
in sober ranks. As for the outgoing
tenant, he too seems unscathed. Seated
cross-legged on top of the cliff, shoulder blades
down and spine erect, he could almost be
one of those limber old dogs who hang around
Wanda, chanting and swallowing twine.

In response to Joe's greeting, he climbs to
his feet. 'Give me a hand here with this, will
you, friend?'
                On the chainsawed stump
of a long-dead tree squats the antique Smith
Corona. Its brass fittings gleam. Just for
a moment Bardruin pauses . . . then levers
it on to his bony knee and indicates
Joe should take one side (the machine, he
discovers, is surprisingly heavy).

Beneath their feet the cliff falls away
precipitously. The ex-poet counts:
one (and swing), two (and swing), three –
and the lumbering beast takes wing, plunges,
snags on a rocky crag, then kicks off (*ping!*
goes the carriage return), tumbling
drunkenly end over end to crash
in a gratifying outburst of spray.
The two men look down at the spot where it
sank, at the blue closing over
dispassionately, until ten seconds later,
with an audible poot, it gives up its mortal
afflatus like a fart in the bath.

Showered, shaved and breakfasted (on a
prodigal helping of Sigrid's pancakes)
Bardruin sets off on sandalled feet to make
the two-mile hike from the Farmhouse to
Marigold's cottage. The autumn morning
is blithe and bonny: he whistles an
intricate, upbeat tune. Welcome swallows
dip round the olives. A kingfisher
eyes him astutely from a telegraph wire.

From the crest of the ridge, the horizon
is cloudless: the Isle of Drunks seems to
float on a cushion of air. Fleetingly
his thoughts turn to Frank, and his book
and the prospect of . . . *No, let it go.*
He nods to occasional passing cars –

he can do this, he's free! – but it's strange:
he'll have to relearn the language.

Here's a familiar face, however:
climbing the track out of Marigold's gully
it's Manfred, reputedly taciturn, and yet
hailing him cheerfully: 'Bardruin! Cometh
the man!'
       'You think?'
              'I know. I've just been
with Marigold. Take it from me, that's a
woman looking forward to seeing you!'

✦

And so the erstwhile poet, with bouncing heart,
begins his descent into paradise.
From the gully below he hears birdsong
and chittering hogs.
          'Chaddie's back! Chaddie's
back!' The greeting catches him unawares.
'Look out! This is your Captain speaking.'
   What?
Oh, you. 'Well, yes, Chuck, good to see you.'

Marigold, hearing the banter, comes brightly
to greet him. 'Arthur Bardruin, I presume!'
'It is I and none other!' 'And about time, too.'

Inside, the house smells of fresh bread and
brain-curdling resins.
           'Good Lord!' He gropes

for the nearest chair and they sit, knee
to knee, at the kitchen table. Taking
the other's amenable hand, Marigold
guides it beneath her dress:
                              'Ooh,' says he,
'it's the girl from Ipanema. Did you
do that for me?' 'I didn't do it for
Chuckles, darling.' 'Hah!' 'I'll tell you what else
I did, I just sold a pound of smoke to Manfred.
And look what he gave me. Remember this?'

Back from the grave, it's their old friend
the Baron de Lustrac. The slim-waisted
bottle, modest and classical, lights up
the kitchen like an amber sun. Marigold
hands him a generous snifter; Bardruin,
gravely, delivers the toast: 'To life beyond
poetry.'
          'Down the hatch.'
                              'Mud in your eye,
cabrón.'
          'Chuck, no one asked you!'

Loosening his shoulders, Bardruin stretches,
tips back his chair with a gratified sigh.
'Do you know what, my dear . . . ?' – *don't
mind if I do*, as his lover re-charges
the brandy balloons, the reek of the weed
harvest commingling sweetly with the woozy
aromas of cloves and burnt sugar –
'somehow I get the distinct impression
this ex-poet's about to make a pig of himself.'

Acknowledgements

The earliest fragments of *Escape Path Lighting* were written while I was Writer in Residence at the University of Waikato in 2014. The bulk of the first draft was written at the University of Canterbury where I held the Ursula Bethell Fellowship in 2017. My sincere thanks to Creative New Zealand, to the two universities and to my departmental colleagues in Hamilton and Christchurch.

I am also more grateful than I can possibly say to the late Llew Summers and to his partner Robyn Webster. I have written of their kindness in my book on Llew's sculpture, but this one, too, has always been for Robyn and Llew.

The narrator, and several of his characters, are inclined to speak in real or approximate quotations. To try to list them all would be ingenuous (poetic language doesn't work that way) and contrary to the spirit of the text. That said, pre-loved materials include the following. The poet acknowledged on p. 20 is Dylan Thomas (*Under Milkwood*). Chuck quotes from *Blue Hawaii* on p. 24 and again on p. 60; on p. 72 he shows off his knowledge of Allen Curnow, and on p. 90, of Marianne Moore. Koro Bill, trying out the Smith Corona (p. 45), quotes faithfully from Shelley ('To a Skylark') and approximately from Joyce (*Ulysses*). The dispute about Hemingway and Zane Grey, alluded to on p. 60, is borrowed from Frank Moorhouse (*The Electrical Experience*). The 'pleasing . . . southern rocker' played by the Phantasmatics on p. 61 is 'Sweet Home Alabama'. Bardruin, apprehended in his creative delirium (p. 88), channels Shelley's 'Ode to the West Wind'; on p. 105 he whistles the bed-measuring duet from *The Marriage of Figaro*; arguing with Joe on p. 128 he appeals to Alan Brunton (the Red Mole manifesto), while Joe counters with *King Lear*. Frank, on p. 148, has been reading either Blake or *Owls Do Cry*; on pp. 150–51 he admires Christo and Jeanne-Claude's *Surrounded Islands*. The poetry-loving biker on p. 164 quotes Robert Creeley. Bardruin, in the preamble to his self-denunciation (pp. 169-70), is trying to remember Cyril Connolly. 'How Blest Are Ye Whose Toils Are Ended' (p. 175) is a Lutheran hymn, written by Simon Dach and translated by Henry Wadsworth Longfellow, and Joe's endearment 'you old disgrace' was bestowed by Conrad Aiken on his protégé Malcolm Lowry.